GOD'S MISSION, MY MISSION

Other books by Gary Krause

God's Great Missionaries

GOD'S MISSION, MY MISSION

Gary Krause

Pacific Press®
Publishing Association
Nampa, Idaho | www.pacificpress.com

Cover design by Brandon Reese
Cover design resources from Lars Justinen

The author assumes full responsibility for the accuracy of all facts and quotations as cited in this book.

To order additional copies of this book or other Sabbath School companion books, please call toll-free 1-800-765-6955, or visit Adventistbookcenter.com.

ISBN 978-0-8163-6924-9

May 2023

Dedication

For Bettina and Bethany, my wife and daughter. Love you forever.

Contents

Preface

One day in 1941, the Swiss engineer George de Mestral was removing burrs that were clinging to his clothes and his dog's fur. They'd been on a hunting trip in the Alps, and de Mestral was fascinated by how the burrs had attached themselves so efficiently. He decided to investigate further. With the help of a microscope, he soon discovered nature's hidden fastening system—hundreds of natural "hooks" on the burrs that latched on to tiny "loops" on things such as fur, socks, and hair.

De Mestral, engineer that he was, decided to try copying the idea. After years of research and development, he invented Velcro, which has now become a multimillion-dollar business. De Mestral reportedly once joked with his executives: "If any of your employees ask for a two-week holiday to go hunting, say yes."

Velcro plagiarizes nature's microscopic system of hooks and loops. It's now used in everything from clothing and gardening to electronics and home decoration. Connecting thousands of hooks and loops creates strong, efficient, and lasting attachments.

Jesus' mission was a Velcro mission, connecting with people at different levels and in different ways. That's what wholistic mission is all about—building strong, multilevel connections through a series of loving "hooks" and "loops." Jesus wasn't content just to share an idea, a one-hook type of mission. His connections were many and stronger, hooking into the loops of people's lives—their physical, mental, spiritual, and emotional needs. These connections drew people to Him and changed their lives for eternity.

As we explore God's mission in this book, I hope we'll also learn more about our mission. We will look at how effective mission studies the "loops" in people's lives and finds connection points. We'll see how a wholistic mission is more than just preaching truth; it's demonstrating truth. It's more than just a series of events; it's an ongoing process. It doesn't just reach people's heads; it touches their hearts. Wholistic mission is driven by the example of the compassionate Jesus who came and dwelled among us.

I'm indebted to many people for helping inspire this book. Thank you, directors of the Global Mission Centers and the rest of the Adventist Mission team. You wrestle every day with finding the best ways to reach diverse people groups around the world. And heartfelt appreciation to you, Bettina and Bethany. Not only are you my best and kindest critics but you've also taught me more theology and missiology than any class or book.

1

God's Mission to Us: Part 1

The lives of Li Jingzhi and Mao Zhenping came crashing down at six o'clock in the evening on October 17, 1988. That's when someone kidnapped their two-year-old son, Mao Yin (nicknamed Jiajia). Mao's father had just picked him up from kindergarten in their home city of Xian, in northwest China. Together they were walking home. Mao asked for a drink, and they stopped in front of the Jinlin Hotel. His father took out a flask with hot water and started to cool it by pouring it between cups. He looked away for a moment and regretted it for the rest of his life.

It's the stuff of every parent's worst nightmare. In a city of some twelve million people, where do you even begin looking? Jiajia's heartbroken mother quit her job and devoted herself full time to searching for her little boy. And so began a quest that went on for more than thirty years. Li distributed more than a hundred thousand flyers in Xian and neighboring provinces. She went on numerous TV programs pleading for help in finding her beloved son. She even started volunteering with Baobei Huijia, which means "baby come home," an organization devoted to helping Chinese families find missing children.

Chinese government restrictions on family size made it even more painful. In the face of exploding growth in the 1960s, the government decreed that all families could have no more than two children. In 1979, seven years before Mao Yin was born, the government reduced it to one child.[1] Li Jingzhi and Mao Zhenping had the added pain of knowing their lost son might be their only child.

"Hope is what motivates me to keep on living," Li said in 2019, after thirty-one years of searching for her son. "People should never lose hope. I believe, someday, I will finally find my son." Li looked into a TV camera and addressed her son, whom she could only hope and pray was still alive and watching. She said: "I hope, Jiajia, you must remember Mom will love you forever. Mom won't give up looking for you. It doesn't matter how you're living, or where you are. You must tell me where you are, just to reassure me. Please don't make me remain uncertain forever. My heart feels the pain. You are thirty-three now. Maybe you are married and have a child of your own. I wouldn't bother you or try to change your life. My only desire is to know that you are still alive where you are."[2]

Unrelenting love

Li's unrelenting search faintly echoes the boundless and relentless compassion of God the Father. From its first pages, the Bible portrays Him as actively searching for His lost children. When Adam and Eve disobeyed, God searched the Garden: "Where are you?" (Genesis 3:9). When Cain's hands dripped with his brother's blood, God called to him, "Where is Abel your brother?" (Genesis 4:9, ESV) You can hear the pain in God's voice: "What have you done? The voice of your brother's blood is crying to me from the ground" (verse 10, ESV). And when Abraham abandoned Hagar and Ishmael alone and without water in the wilderness, "God heard the boy crying" (Genesis 21:17). God remains closely attuned to His creation. He listens, watches, feels, and responds.

God heard His people crying in Egypt (Exodus 3:7). He saw baby Moses floating in a makeshift boat on the Nile River. He saw an Egyptian princess adopt him. And He saw Moses ascend to power and influence in Pharaoh's court. He also saw his dramatic fall and found him shepherding, hidden in what the Bible calls the "backside of the desert" (verse 1, KJV). It was quite a change of pace for Moses, a prince who had once walked the majestic hallways of Pharaoh's palace. God called to him by name through the burning bush: "Moses! Moses!" (verse 4).

Through the years, people have tried to explain away the burning bush. Charles Baukal Jr. summarizes some of the theories: "Hallucinogenic drugs, an active volcano, optical illusions, natural gas leak, subterranean fire, St. Elmo's fire, a bush with red berries or flowers, and a bush that emitted flammable vapors."[3] Any reader unable to accept the burning bush as a supernatural encounter would be shocked by the rest of Moses' story!

Through the miraculous burning bush, God reached out to Moses and assured him of His unceasing care for His people. He again revealed Himself as the God intimately connected with His creation. He sees ("I have surely seen the affliction of my people who are in Egypt" [verse 7, ESV]), hears ("[I] have heard their cry" [verse 7, ESV]), and understands ("I know their sufferings" [verse 7, ESV]). Then He called Moses to action.

The Bible says that the "backside of the desert" where God found Moses was Mount Horeb, "the mountain of God" (verse 1). Also known as Mount Sinai, it's where Moses would later receive the Ten Commandments, the "living words" of God's law (Acts 7:38). It's also where, many years later, God finds another prophet, Elijah. Unlike Moses, Elijah wasn't tending sheep. Elijah, the mighty prophet of God, was cowering in a cave.

This is one of the beautiful things about the Bible. It tells the truth about people. It doesn't shine its heroes and heroines with false spiritual polish, glossing over their faults and mistakes. Think for a moment about Elijah. He was just coming off an unbelievable mountaintop experience on Mount Carmel. The lone prophet of God had faced off against 450 prophets of Baal in a literal trial by fire. He laughed at them, made jokes about them, and taunted them. You get the feeling that Elijah enjoyed every second of the experience. God spectacularly rewarded his faith and showed who was in charge. But then everything went downhill, so to speak. Elijah ran to Jezreel. It may have been downhill, but it was still the length of a modern marathon and an impressive effort for a prophet after a long day on the mountain.

From here, the script reads more like a roller coaster. In Jezreel, Elijah received a menacing message from Queen Jezebel, threatening to kill him. Elijah ran again, this time for his life. He eventually reached Beersheba and then headed into the wilderness. Finally, he slumped under a juniper tree and prayed that he might die: "It is enough; now, O LORD, take away my life; for I am no better than my fathers" (1 Kings 19:4, ESV).

It was a stunning fall, emotionally, physically, and spiritually. On Mount Carmel, Elijah could scarcely contain his joy as he mocked the priests of Baal. He triumphed as God's fire consumed the altars and smoke billowed into the heavens. But in the end, he hid under a juniper tree, wanting to die.

Mood and food

Emotional and spiritual highs followed by low points, even despair, are part of being human. Swimmer Michael Phelps, the greatest Olympian of all time, estimates that 80 percent of athletes experience post-Olympic depression of one kind or another. Over his Olympic career, Phelps won twenty-eight Olympic medals, including twenty-three golds. It's a medal tally for a single athlete that's higher than the total tally of many countries. And yet he suffered crippling depression. "Really, after every Olympics I think I fell into a major state of depression," he told the fourth annual conference of the Kennedy Forum. After the 2012 Olympics, where he won four gold and two silver medals, he stayed in his bedroom, not wanting to eat and hardly sleeping.[4] "It was October of 2014 that I lost all hope," he said in a TV commercial. "I was one of the world's most successful athletes. Eighteen gold medals, the all-American dream come true. But I was lost. I hadn't left my room in five days. I questioned whether I wanted to be alive anymore."[5]

We celebrate the mountaintop achievements of elite athletes. But less-publicized mountaintop experiences happen every day. Emergency room physicians work around the clock, scarcely taking a breath between patients. Teachers tirelessly invest in the lives of their students. Pastors engage in intense church activities over the weekend—organizing, meeting people, preaching. All are susceptible to some sort of "crash" when it's over. Psychologist Archibald Hart calls this "postadrenaline depression," in which stress depletes a person's supply of adrenaline. "[Pastors] succumb to postadrenaline depression on Mondays when their adrenal system crashes and demands time for recovery," he writes. "They may feel depressed, irritable, and negative about everything."[6] In other words, please cut your pastor some slack on Monday mornings.

God found Elijah under the juniper tree and sent an angel to feed him. God was concerned about something as mundane as Elijah's eating habits. He knew that proper food would help revive him and rally his spirits. "Put simply, what you eat directly affects the structure and function of your brain and, ultimately, your mood," writes Dr. Eva Selhub from Harvard Medical School. Selhub compares the brain to an expensive car, which functions best on premium fuel. Premium fuels for the brain are foods high in vitamins, minerals, and antioxidants. Cheap fuel, which can damage the brain and adversely affect its mood, are processed foods and foods high in refined sugars. "What's interesting is that for many years, the medical field did not fully acknowledge the connection between mood and food," Selhub says.[7] But God knew the connection. Whatever delicacy the angel served Elijah, it energized him to keep heading into the wilderness for forty days and nights until he reached Mount Horeb.

But once again, Elijah's energy was spent, and this time God found him huddling in a cave. Dread and loneliness had replaced the spiritual and emotional high of Mount Carmel.

God gently asked him, "What are you doing here, Elijah?" (1 Kings 19:9, NRSV). It's a simple question that probes the heart of his situation. Note that Elijah expresses no shock at hearing God's voice. He doesn't exclaim, "Who is this?" He knows God, and he knows God's voice. And he answers, "I have been very zealous for the LORD, the God of hosts; for the Israelites have forsaken your covenant, thrown down your altars, and killed your prophets with the sword. I alone am left, and they are seeking my life, to take it away" (verse 10, NRSV).

God dazzles with another Mount Carmel–like experience with wind, earthquake, and fire. He whispers the question again, "What are you doing here, Elijah?" (verse 13, NRSV). Elijah gives an identical reply. This time God assures Elijah that he's not alone. In fact, he's one of seven thousand faithful believers still living in Israel. And He gives Elijah a to-do list that will keep him busy and distract him from his malaise (verses 14–18).

Elijah was blessed. During every step of his physical and emotional journey, God was watching over him. God knew where he was. There was nowhere he could turn where God wouldn't find him.

Bringing back the strays

Centuries after Elijah, the Jewish exiles felt that their God had abandoned them. Babylon's armies had destroyed their temple. They'd lost their beloved Jerusalem and were captives in a pagan land. But God was watching and planning for their deliverance. On one level, the Babylonians were responsible for the exile. They sacked Jerusalem, looted the city, and exiled the captives to Babylon. But the prophet Ezekiel, one of the exiles, blamed Judah's leaders. He rebuked them as shepherds who cared more about themselves than their sheep. "You have not strengthened the weak, you have not healed the sick, you have not bound up the injured, you have not brought back the strayed, you have not sought the lost, but with force and harshness you have ruled them" (Ezekiel 34:4, NRSV). Ezekiel here describes spiritual shepherds who were not pastoral and who did not care for the sheep who had strayed. And the sheep certainly had strayed: "My sheep were scattered over all the face of the earth, with none to search or seek for them" (verse 6, ESV).

In the face of the spectacular, self-indulgent failure of the leaders, God announced that He would step in and become their Shepherd: "I myself will search for my sheep and look after them. . . . I will search for the lost and bring back the strays. I will bind up the injured and strengthen the weak" (Ezekiel 34:11–16). Isaiah says,

> "He will tend his flock like a shepherd;
>> he will gather the lambs in his arms,
> he will carry them in his bosom,
>> and gently lead those that are with young" (Isaiah 40:11, ESV).

In other words, God will do what the spiritual leaders should have done.

Ezekiel portrays God as doing two things in His role as missionary Shepherd. The two Hebrew words he uses, *darash* and *baqar*, both convey the meaning of *seeking* and *searching* (Ezekiel 34:11). But *baqar* can add the extra sense of making concerned inquiries. It's as if God Himself goes searching for the sheep and, on the way, knocks on people's doors to ask if they've seen His lost sheep.

In Jeremiah's time, God promised Israel, "I will give you shepherds after my own heart" (Jeremiah 3:15). It's in the heart of God to be a Shepherd who seeks His sheep and feeds them with "knowledge and understanding" (verse 15).

The Good Shepherd

Centuries later, Jesus came as a searching, inquiring Shepherd. He

called Himself the Good Shepherd. He knows His sheep, leaves the fold
to find and gather them, and even lays down His life for them (John
10:14–16). He's the Shepherd who leaves the ninety-nine sheep to find
the one lost sheep (Luke 15:3–6).

Shepherds in Bible times knew their sheep. "Responsible shepherds
know every member of their flocks in terms of their birth circumstances,
history of health, eating habits and other idiosyncrasies. It is not uncom-
mon to name each goat and sheep and to call them by name (John
10:3ff.)."[8] In Jesus' parable of the lost sheep, the shepherd searches for
a sheep that he probably knows well—even though it's just one out of
a hundred. He knows when and where the lamb was born and what it
likes to eat; but most important, he knows it by name. You can picture
the Shepherd heading into the wilderness, calling, "Daisy! Daisy! Daisy!"
Or whatever name that they gave sheep back then.

The way Matthew tells it, the Shepherd gets more joy in finding the lost
sheep than He does in the ninety-nine that never went astray (Matthew
18:13). Luke's account extends the joy even wider to describe "more joy
in heaven" (Luke 15:7, ESV). It's not that the Shepherd doesn't care for
and love the ninety-nine. It's just that there's an elevated level of joy in
finding the lost sheep, lifting it onto His shoulders, and bringing it home.
And when the Shepherd gets home in triumph with His lost sheep, He
calls his friends and neighbors to celebrate (verse 6).

Of course, this parable isn't really about the lost sheep. Daisy, bless
her heart, doesn't know much about what's going on. It's all about the
Shepherd who cares for her, sacrifices to save her, and rejoices when He
gets her home with Him where she belongs.

A Greek or Roman of the time would have found this picture of God
absurd. Their gods displayed human emotions on steroids. They were
powerful, immoral, and totally unpredictable. They certainly interfered
in the lives of human beings, but not with the personalized care and
compassion of the Good Shepherd. We're told that when Jesus looked at

18

the crowds, He looked at them with compassion because they were "like sheep without a shepherd" (Matthew 9:36). The Greek gods never looked at people with compassion. And the ancients certainly couldn't imagine Zeus or Apollo or Poseidon combing through the wilderness, searching for a lost sheep.

"The simple phrase 'For God so loved the world . . .' would have puzzled an educated pagan," writes sociologist Rodney Stark. "And the notion that the gods care how we treat one another would have been dismissed as patently absurd." The concept of a God loving human beings who, in return, love Him back was a foreign concept in the Roman world. In classical philosophy, mercy and pity were defects of character. In the ideal state that Plato described, the best way to deal with beggars was to dump them outside the borders of the nation-state.[9]

But in Jesus, we see a Shepherd who cares for the discarded of society. He heals lepers, the lame, and the demon-possessed. He's the One who seeks and saves the lost.

The lost are found

In 2020, Li Jingzhi's hopes and prayers were answered. On May 10, Mother's Day in China, she learned her son had been found—alive and well—in another province. Eight long days later, parents and child were reunited, duly recorded by television cameras, in a moment that would bring tears to even the most hardened eyes. As mother, father, and son hugged each other, it was clear that more than three decades of searching was worth it all. "I don't want him to leave me anymore," said Li Jingzhi, clinging to her son's hand. "I won't let him leave me anymore."[10]

---

1. The policy was more relaxed for parents in rural areas. If their first child was a girl, they were permitted to have a second child. The policy was abolished in 2015.

2. Lea Li and Andersen Xia, "Kidnapped: The Chinese Parents Desperately Searching for Missing Children," *South China Morning Post*, January 14, 2020, https://www.scmp.com/video/scmp-films/3046029/kidnapped-chinese-parents-desperately-searching-missing-children?utm_source=Yahoo&utm_medium=partner&utm_content=3084925&utm_campaign=contentexchange; Nectar Gan, "Facial Recognition Helps Reunite Kidnapped Toddler With Family After 32 Years," CNN, May 19, 2020, https://www.cnn.com/2020/05/19/asia/china-kidnapped-son-reunited-intl-hnk/indExodushtml; "China Abductions: Parents Find Son Snatched in Hotel 32 Years Ago," BBC, May 19, 2020, https://www.bbc.com/news/world-asia-china-52717670.

3. Charles E. Baukal, "Pyrophany on Mount Horeb: The Burning Bush," abstract, *Scandinavian Journal of the Old Testament* 30, no. 2 (2016): 215–235.

4. Susan Scutti, "Michael Phelps: 'I Am Extremely Thankful That I Did Not Take My Life,'" CNN, January 20, 2018, https://www.cnn.com/2018/01/19/health/michael-phelps-depression/.

5. Talkspace, "Talkspace x Michael Phelps: How Therapy Helped Save His Life," YouTube video, 0:45, May 22, 2018, https://www.youtube.com/watch?v=j7KuJJruD4o.

6. Archibald D. Hart, *Unmasking Male Depression* (Nashville, TN: Thomas Nelson, 2000), 42.

7. Eva Selhub, "Nutritional Psychiatry: Your Brain on Food," Harvard Health Publishing, September 18, 2022, https://www.health.harvard.edu/blog/nutritional-psychiatry-your-brain-on-food-201511168626.

8. Timothy S. Laniak, *Shepherds After My Own Heart: Pastoral Traditions and Leadership in the Bible*, New Studies in Biblical Theology, vol. 20, ed. D. A. Carson (Downers Grove, IL: InterVarsity, 2015), 57.

9. Rodney Stark, *The Rise of Christianity* (Princeton, NJ: Princeton University Press, 1996), 211, 212.

10. Cindy Sui, "It Took 32 Years, but I Finally Found My Kidnapped Son," BBC.com, August 7, 2020, https://www.bbc.com/news/stories-53566460.

2

God's Mission to Us: Part 2

Football, or soccer as some know it, is wildly popular. No other sporting event attracts as many viewers as the World Cup, which is held every four years. An estimated 715 million people watched the 2006 World Cup final between Italy and France. That's the equivalent of every person in Western Europe, the United States, South Africa, Argentina, South Korea, and Canada tuning in to watch the game. Within twenty minutes of the referee's opening whistle, both sides scored. France's goal came first from star midfielder Zinedine Zidane's penalty kick in the seventh minute. Eight years earlier, Zidane had led France to victory in the World Cup Final against Brazil. Now he seemed poised to do it again against Italy.

Despite the frenetic start, the match was still drawn at one goal each at the end of ninety minutes, forcing extra time. Then, with just ten minutes remaining, something extraordinary happened. The great Zidane walked over to Italian defender Marco Materazzi and viciously headbutted him in the chest. Materazzi went down, the referee's red card went up, and Zidane was sent off. It ended his professional playing career.

Football fans and experts have endlessly dissected, discussed, and debated the incident. Armchair experts have viewed and reviewed it millions and millions of times on YouTube. Reportedly, Zidane was responding to a personal insult from Materazzi. Serious football fans can describe his rich legacy as a player and can recite his numerous triumphs on the field. But the rest of us, if we even recognize his name, remember only the headbutt—his final and most memorable moment as a professional player.

Whatever the explanations and justifications, that headbutt meant France played the last ten minutes of the game with one less player on the field. One undisciplined moment robbed the French team of their best player for the ten most crucial minutes of the game. Zidane's exit was sad, it was pathetic, and it may have been the key factor in France missing another World Cup victory. Italy won in a 5–3 penalty shoot-out.

The power of choice

Zidane's red card reminds us that all actions have consequences, whether played out in front of 715 million people, in the school or workplace, or in the privacy of our homes. Adam and Eve walked and talked with God, but when they disobeyed Him, they received a red card and exited the Garden of Eden. Moses was a mighty prophet and friend of God, but when he disobeyed God at the waters of Meribah Kadesh, God gave him a red card—he would not enter the Promised Land (Numbers 20:10–12; Deuteronomy 32:51, 52).

Years later, Judas Iscariot also earned a red card. "Keeper of the money bag" (John 12:6) for Jesus and the other disciples, he presented a false face of piety. Once, he expressed outrage when Mary anointed Jesus with expensive perfume. He muttered, "Why wasn't this perfume sold and the money given to the poor? It was worth a year's wages" (verse 5). In case anyone might be tempted to agree, John gives the backstory: "He did not say this because he cared about the poor but because he was a thief" (verse 6). The seemingly pious Judas dipped into the funds whenever he felt like it.

Judas finally betrayed Jesus with a kiss in the Garden of Gethsemane (Matthew 26:47–49). His traitorous actions explain why Judas doesn't top the list of favorite baby names. To Jesus, that kiss, now symbolic of the deepest treachery, must have felt like a headbutt to the chest. Sent from the field, Judas hung himself, and as a result, Matthew wrote one of the saddest verses in the Bible: "Now the eleven disciples went to Galilee, to the mountain to which Jesus had directed them" (Matthew 28:16, ESV). Once there were twelve disciples. Now they were one player short because of a fateful kiss.

Jesus had spent three and a half years mentoring Judas. Judas had heard Jesus say, "Come unto me, all ye that labour and are heavy laden, and I will give you rest" (Matthew 11:28, KJV). He had heard Jesus say, "I am the way, and the truth, and the life" (John 14:6, KJV). He had seen Jesus heal lepers, raise the dead, and weep over Jerusalem. Now Judas was dead.

Only eleven disciples made the journey to Galilee, to the mountain where Jesus had told them to go (Matthew 28:16), the place where they would receive their mission statement, establishing God's church on Earth. A mission statement Judas would never get to hear. A church he would never get to see.

Disqualified

The shell-shocked group of disciples, short one player, gathered to meet Jesus. They thought they had known Judas. Yes, he'd betrayed Jesus, but in a sense, he'd betrayed them all. Even worse, each of them knew that they, too, were guilty. Each of them "forsook him, and fled" (Matthew 26:56, KJV). Each of them betrayed Jesus in their own way, casting Him aside when He didn't have a friend. Now He was leaving them, and they didn't know what to do.

When the disciples saw the resurrected Jesus, they worshiped Him.

And yet, in this time of supercharged emotion, as they stood on the mountain with Jesus right in front of them, some still doubted (Matthew 28:17). Let's be clear about what happens next. It's a pivotal moment in history. Jesus entrusts His mission of salvation to a spiritually wounded team, a team of uneducated, bickering, cowardly, ambitious, theologically confused, doubting, and unfaithful men. Anyone looking on would exclaim, "Good luck with that!"

From a human standpoint, it's baffling. How could He trust these eleven men? They lacked faith, misunderstood His teachings, jockeyed for position, and abandoned Him when He needed them most. And yet, Jesus commissioned them as His ambassadors on Earth.

This is good news for us today. Jesus specializes in calling the damaged, the weak, and the unfaithful. We may feel ill-equipped, unprepared, and unworthy of being involved in God's mission, but Jesus still calls us. In fact, He finds it harder to call those who feel they're worthy, those who feel they're doing Jesus a favor by offering Him all their skills, charisma, and talent.

There they stood, a group of eleven broken men. And yet Jesus gave them the gospel commission. Often, we quote only part of this commission, neglecting what Jesus says at the beginning and the end. The commission really starts with these words: "Then Jesus came to them and said, 'All authority in heaven and on earth has been given to me' " (Matthew 28:18). This is the context in which Jesus frames His commission. And it's vitally important for His depleted, fragile, confused followers to hear that. He then adds, "Therefore, go . . ." (verse 19). It's because the One who has "all authority in heaven and on earth" is with them that they will be able to go into all the world. The only reason this wounded team of eleven men can even think of going is that they're going in Jesus' power. In the same way, the final words of the commission are just as important: "And surely I am with you always, to the very end of the age" (verse 20). The commission is bookended by reassurance. They could go in Jesus' authority (verse 18), knowing that He would be with them all the way (verse 20).

The Great Commission

Today, we take it for granted that the Great Commission applies to us, not just the first disciples. But that view wasn't always the case. In 1786, a group of Baptist pastors met in Northampton, England. The chairman of the meeting, Dr. Ryland, invited the young pastors present to suggest topics for discussion. No doubt feeling a bit intimidated, no one replied. Finally, after some encouragement, one of them asked "whether the command given to the Apostles, to teach all nations, was not obligatory on all succeeding ministers to the end of the world, seeing that the accompanying promise was of equal extent." Ryland reportedly shouted a rebuke: "You are a miserable enthusiast for asking such a question."[1] According to some accounts, he added, "When God pleases to convert the heathen, he'll do it without consulting you or me."

The young man scolded for asking the question that evening was William Carey. Undeterred, six years later, in 1792, he wrote a watershed pamphlet entitled *Enquiry Into the Obligations of Christians, to Use Means for the Conversion of the Heathens*. Why was the pamphlet a watershed? Because the dominant view of Christians at the time, as demonstrated by Ryland, was that the Great Commission was only for the eleven disciples. In his pamphlet, Carey describes the prevailing view he was attacking: "It is thus that multitudes sit at ease, and give themselves no concern about the far greater part of their fellow-sinners, who to this day, are lost in ignorance and idolatry."[2]

In 1792, largely due to Carey's influence, what's now known as the Baptist Missionary Society was founded. The binding nature of the Great Commission wasn't just an abstract theory or theological argument for Carey. The following year he and his family boarded a ship as missionaries to India. Serving there for forty-one years without a furlough, Carey experienced heartache and joy. His five-year-old son died from dysentery. His wife plunged into a permanent mental breakdown before dying in 1807. The record is clear that Carey was so driven by his calling that sometimes his family suffered. He wasn't perfect, but his vision of mission was strong. He worked tirelessly for the well-being and eternal welfare of the Indian people. Today, he's often called the father of modern Protestant missions.

Carey lived his beliefs. In 1835, the *Family Magazine* of London published a copy of his last will. The editors stated, "It will be seen that . . . he could bequeath his children little else than his library, and the benefit of his great example." Carey also directed the words he wanted to be inscribed on his tomb:

William Carey, born August 17, 1761,
  died ———
A wretched, poor, and helpless worm,
  On thy kind arms I fall.[3]

Carey's life and influence prepared the way for Protestant mission work and, in turn, the later mission of the Seventh-day Adventist Church.

Subversive words

As Jesus gathered those eleven disciples together, little did they imagine the import of His commission. Those words would continue to serve as the rallying call for the mission of the Christian church two thousand years later. But at the time, any Roman who happened to overhear those final words of Jesus would have considered them subversive. Statements such as "all authority in heaven and on earth has been given to me" would have sounded like sedition (Matthew 28:18). When Jesus said this, Rome was occupying Judea, and the emperor cult was at its peak. "Virgil, Josephus and other writers claimed that Rome was actually divinely commissioned to expand power over all the nations."[4] One of the titles for Roman emperors was "savior of the world," and writers of the time described Rome as having a divine commission to go into all the world.

But Jesus commissioned His disciples to spread the good news of salvation, not Roman power. It's not a gospel of power and force but a gospel of love, hope, and compassion. They didn't go in the power of any earthly government or authority but under the banner of the One who has "all authority in heaven and on earth." They were to make disciples in the name of the One who has more authority than any Roman emperor could even dream about.

Jesus the Shepherd

In stark contrast to the might of Rome, Jesus ushered in a new way of seeing the world. He came to Earth so that he could "seek and save the lost" (Luke 19:10). He found and ministered to a Samaritan woman by Jacob's well in the town of Sychar (John 4:4–42). He found and healed blind Bartimaeus beside the road, just outside Jericho (Mark 10:46–52). And while passing through Jericho, he found a tax collector up in a sycamore tree (Luke 19:1–10). Pausing beneath that tree, Jesus looked up and saw Zacchaeus perched on a branch. Luke describes Zacchaeus searching, seeking, inquiring—trying to find out who Jesus was (verse 3). A seeker met the Seeker. He soon learned about Jesus in a way that he never anticipated. Jesus told Zacchaeus He wanted to visit his home.

As a side note, Luke says that the people watching the encounter murmured and muttered among themselves (verse 7). The Greek word he uses, *diagoggýzon*, is onomatopoeic. In other words, when spoken, the word sounds exactly like what it means—"buzzing like bees." Here the people were bees buzzing in disapproval. How could Jesus visit the home of such a notorious sinner as Zacchaeus? Didn't He know his sordid story? Luke uses the same Greek word earlier in his book to describe the outraged teachers of the law and Pharisees when they see Jesus mixing and eating with sinners. They *diagoggýzon* about the fact that "this man welcomes sinners and eats with them" (Luke 15:2).

After Jesus invites Himself to Zacchaeus's house, the rest of the story happens behind closed doors. But whatever Jesus did, whatever He said, life was never the same for Zacchaeus. He announced, "Behold, Lord, the half of my goods I give to the poor. And if I have defrauded anyone of anything, I restore it fourfold," (Luke 19:8, ESV). And Jesus' summary? "Today salvation has come to this house" (verse 9, ESV). Once again, Jesus demonstrated His mission "to seek and to save the lost" (verse 10, ESV).

The Greek word translated here as "lost," *apolōlos*, has as its root meaning "destruction." Zacchaeus had been traveling down a dangerous and destructive pathway. He loved his bank account more than his neighbors. He was lost in badly misguided priorities. Because of Jesus, he repents, which literally means he turns around. He starts walking on a fresh path of healing and salvation. Jesus had liberated Zacchaeus into a new and more abundant life.

The Zacchaeus story reminds us that there are various forms of lostness. A person can possess an expensive house and a full investment portfolio yet have an empty life. The searching Savior came to fill empty lives.

The lost are now found

In answer to the religious leaders buzzing like bees about His association with "sinners," Jesus told three stories about being lost—the lost sheep, the lost coin, and the lost son (Luke 15). Remembering that the Greek word for "lost" has the root meaning of "destruction" adds an edge to these stories. The sheep wasn't only lost; she faced all sorts of mortal peril outside the safety of the sheepfold (verse 4). Likewise, the coin's value was destroyed while it hid in a dusty corner somewhere (verse 8). And the lostness of the son, partying in a far country, took on a dangerous, more destructive turn when his money and his friends ran out. He was forced to deny his religious-cultural heritage and identity by working in a pigpen just to survive (verses 13–15). A Jewish boy working in a pigpen would be like an Adventist boy serving cocktails in a bar.

The pivotal moment was when he "came to himself" and realized he'd be better off even as a servant in his father's house (verse 17, KJV). He headed for home in great shame, with no idea of the depth of his father's unconditional love. On the way home, he practiced his speech—"Father, I have sinned against heaven and before you" (verse 18, ESV).

I imagine the son with nicotine stains on his fingers, alcohol on his breath, and the smell of dope in his hair, still stinking of pigs. His father probably smelled him before he saw him. And no doubt his father, freshly washed, was wearing a fresh, clean garment. But, seeing his son coming from a far distance, he ran, robes flowing in the wind, to embrace him. It was an undignified way for a man of his distinction to behave.

The son tried his speech. He started off strongly: "Father, I have sinned against heaven and before you. I am no longer worthy to be called your son" (verse 21, ESV). But right there, before he could say another word, his father cut him off. He didn't get to finish. His father had no interest in hearing it. He was too busy rejoicing that his son was home. At that moment, the son began to shed his lostness and bask in the sunshine of being where he truly belonged (verses 17–22).

I imagine the son looked skinny and sick from the nutritional limitations of eating pig fodder. Not exactly five servings of fruit and vegetables per day. Alarmed, the father immediately commanded his servants to prepare the fatted calf. But the command was about more than just feeding a hungry boy. It meant that the father would eat and celebrate at the table with his son. And more than that, he would give him a ring for his finger and fresh garments to wear, symbolizing celebration, acceptance, realignment, and a fresh start (verses 22–24). The father had found his lost son.

In these stories, Jesus richly illustrated what He called the "good news of the kingdom" (Luke 4:43). It's the good news that He commissioned His disciples to share with all the world. It's the good news our world still needs to hear.

The joy of being found

Recently I saw a social media post on a neighborhood message board. It said:

Lost Dog. My sweet Olive is still missing! She is wearing a light blue collar! Please continue to keep an eye out for her. If you see her, please call [*XXX-XXX-XXXX*] or send me a PM IMMEDIATELY! . . . . Please do not call or chase her. She is very scared and will run. She disappeared from our home on Wild Grass Ct. on Jan. 29.

Soon there was an avalanche of replies:

"I will keep an eye out for your sweet girl."

"My heart goes out to u; my eyes are alert."

"Will definitely be on the lookout for her."

"I'm sorry she's still missing. I'll keep my eyes open when I'm around that area. I hope she turns up soon!!"

"I hope you find her soon. I know how hard it is to have pets lost."

"I'm sorry. You must be heartbroken. Hoping for the best."

A few days later, the neighbor posted the good news:

Olive has been found! I want to thank everyone so much for their thoughts and prayers and for all of the tips you've given to us over these past 8 days. A wonderful couple found her under their neighbor's deck. She is skinny and has a limp, but is in good shape otherwise. She's at the Pet ER being checked out now.

Then the neighbors started to rejoice:

"Wow! SO glad."

"That's great news! Thank you for letting your neighbors know!"

"I am so happy to read this update! I was praying for an update like this one."

"Yay!!! I've been thinking about her. So glad this story has a happy ending and that now she can start her life as part of your family!"

"You've had a lot of followers praying for her safe return. Bravo!"

"Hurray."

"Oh, what great news!"

"Oh, thank goodness! My kids have been so concerned and looking anywhere they went. Welcome home, Olive!"

And the online rejoicing went on and on. It was like Luke 15 all over again. The lost are found. Neighbors celebrate. Heaven rejoices.

---

1. George Smith, *The Life of William Carey, D.D.: Shoemaker and Missionary* (London: John Murray, 1885), 31.

2. William Carey, *An Enquiry Into the Obligations of Christians, to Use Means for the Conversion of the Heathens* (Leicester, England: Ann Ireland, 1792), 8.

3. "Domestic and Foreign Intelligence: India," *Family Magazine* 2, no. 8 (January 1835): 29, https://www.google.com/books/edition/The_Family_magazine_conducted _by_J_Belch/U20EAAAAQAAJ.

4. Darren Cronshaw, "A Commission 'Great' for Whom? Postcolonial Contrapuntal Readings of Matthew 28:18–20 and the Irony of William Carey," *Transformation* 33, no. 2 (April 2016): 111.

3

God's Call to Mission

On June 3, 2017, Alex Honnold climbed the infamous El Capitan, a majestic three-thousand-foot cliff in America's Yosemite National Park. Only a few elite climbers can make the climb, but Honnold went a monumental step further. He did it free solo, meaning he climbed without any ropes or protective equipment. In other words, one slip, and he would fall. In his understated way, Honnold called it a "high-consequence" endeavor.[1]

Daniel Duane, writing in the *New York Time*, was more effusive, describing it "as one of the great athletic feats of any kind, ever." He wrote that every climber "recognizes it [El Capitan] as the indispensable cliff." He added, "No cliff anywhere combines such unrelenting steepness, glassy smoothness and inspiring immensity—horizontal as well as vertical—with a quality of such coherent unity, of being a single solid object so gigantic as to reliably induce a tingling awareness of creation's incomprehensible mystery."[2]

Honnold's free-solo climb took three hours and fifty-six minutes. That means that for nearly four hours he climbed with every nerve and muscle taut, his mind relentlessly focused on finding the next hint of a foothold or the next fissure he could trust for his fingertips. One mistake, one misplaced finger, and he would plummet to his death. Duane concluded,

"[It was] a performance so far beyond our current understanding of our physical and mental potential that it provokes a pleasurable sensation of mystified awe right alongside the inevitable nausea."[3]

Eight years earlier, another professional climber, Dean Potter, prepared for a different alpine feat. High in the Swiss mountains, he donned a specially designed wingsuit that made him look like some sort of human bat. He then jumped off a cliff nine thousand feet high. With webbed arms outstretched, he flew for two minutes and fifty seconds, covering more than four miles. It was the longest BASE jump, leaping from a fixed object, ever recorded.[4]

BASE jumping competes with free-solo climbing for the dubious privilege of being the most dangerous sport in the world. It's illegal in many places. A former National Geographic Adventurer of the Year, Potter also enjoyed rock climbing and highlining—walking across ropes slung over dangerously high drops. Unsurprisingly, he and a friend died in 2015 while BASE jumping in Yosemite, where Honnold made his record climb.

Comfort zones

Extreme adventurers revel in moving outside their comfort zones and pushing their physical and mental limits. In 1908, psychologists Robert Yerkes and John Dodson tested the relationship between stress and performance. Their research resulted in the Yerkes-Dodson law. It says that when people are operating in their comfort zone, they'll perform consistently at a certain level. But to get beyond that level, to improve their performance, they need to move outside their comfort zone. Not too far, or their performance will fail, but just enough to push them to a higher level. They called that performance sweet spot the level of *optimal anxiety*. It's as if hardships, danger, and stress act as catalysts for better performance.

As Christians, it's easy to settle into a spiritual comfort zone that's really a spiritual danger zone. That's what happened to the church in Laodicea. It became tepid, lukewarm in its faith. God said it would have been better for them to be hot or cold (Revelation 3:15). Instead of scaling mountain heights, the church had become content with playing harmless indoor games. Instead of boldly engaging in mission, it majored in maintenance.

Sociologists can tell us a few things about being lukewarm. American sociologist Peter Berger wrote about what he called "plausibility structures," social structures that support different worldviews and help them make sense.[5] Different societies have various "plausibility structures" that make it easier to believe certain things. Adventist plausibility structures include such things as Sabbath School, church, family, and friends.

Berger argues that any belief or way of life needs a supportive community or group to sustain it. It's generally easier, for example, to keep your faith on a university campus where teachers are believers and you can live, work, and study with committed Christians. It's harder, but not impossible, to sustain an active Christian faith in Iran or Saudi Arabia.

Many Christians spend six days a week buried in the world's values— entertainment, radio talk shows, and social media, where faith is either attacked or ignored. They surround themselves with plausibility structures that support nonbelief. No sociologist would be surprised when their faith turns lukewarm. Such a result is almost inevitable when you limit your Christian experience to a weekend "add-on" called church, a mere extra to your "real" life where God plays no role.

Although plausibility structures support faith, spiritual growth often happens when those structures are tested or weakened. When I was studying at the University of Newcastle in Australia, one of my majors was philosophy. I remember well the first day of one of my classes. The professor walked into the room and said, "I think it's important that you understand where I come from. I used to be a lay preacher with the Methodist Church, but now I'm an atheist. But please understand that I don't think atheism needs any missionaries." Other lecturers weren't so kind and happily attacked Christianity. They undermined the plausibility structures that had surrounded me all my life.

Obviously, an environment in which professors weaken your plausibility structures will challenge your faith more than a place that affirms and supports your faith. But when pushed out of your comfort zone and forced to struggle with what you believe, you may actually strengthen your faith.

This doesn't negate the value of Adventist education. Adventist schools play a vital role in building strong plausibility structures that strengthen and support faith. But effective Adventist education also equips and inspires students to move outside their comfort zones, to become involved in mission and service, where real spiritual growth takes place.

The church in Ephesus had a sickness similar to that of Laodicea. It had lost its first love. Fortunately, the Lord gives the cure: "Work as you did at first" (see Revelation 2:5). He doesn't say to study more, although that's important. He doesn't say to go to church more, although that's important. He doesn't even say to pray more, although that's also important. Rather, Jesus says to work. There's something spiritually vital about action and involvement. "Do not waste time bothering whether you 'love' your neighbour; act as if you did. As soon as we do this, we find one of the great secrets. When you are behaving as if you loved someone, you will presently come to love him."[6] Rediscovering our first love requires action, not just contemplation. Has your first love grown cold? Start acting like a Christian again!

Jesus tells the church in Sardis, "Awake, and strengthen what remains" (Revelation 3:2, RSV). There are times when we feel there's not much remaining. We feel burned out and weak in our faith, with not much left to cling to. But we need to hold on to the remnants of our faith, "what remains," and grip them like life rafts. Then we need to rediscover the things we used to do when we first came to Jesus. Did we spend time in Bible study and prayer? Well, let's start doing that again. Did we share Jesus and His love with others? Let's start that again. Did we have a small-group Bible study? Let's revive that. Did we volunteer time to help people in the community? It's time to volunteer again. Work as you did at first.

Ellen White tells the story of a man near death in a snowstorm. Exhausted, he was about to give up the struggle for life. But then he heard the moans of a fellow traveler. He found the man and instinctively started chafing his frozen limbs. Finally, he got him to stand but discovered he couldn't walk. So he picked him up and carried him through the snow to safety. "The truth flashed home to him that in saving his neighbor," White says, "he had saved himself also."[7] In making the effort to save someone else, he kept himself alive. Mission—pushing ourselves out of our comfort zones for Jesus—revives us.

Legacy of mission

The Seventh-day Adventist Church has a rich legacy of people pushing out of their comfort zones for Jesus. In 1901, Adventist pioneer Stephen Haskell and his wife, Hetty, moved to the heart of New York City. Haskell, at sixty-eight, was a senior Adventist statesman, a close friend of Ellen White, and someone who'd lived most of his life in rural areas. Now, at the start of a new century, the Haskells were thrust into the heart of densely populated New York City.

It was an urban mission field. They moved into the Windermere—a recently built Renaissance revival tenement building. Nearby, trains rushed past on the Ninth Avenue Elevated railroad. Five minutes' walk away was the southwest corner of Central Park. The Haskells seemed a little overwhelmed by the city, almost fearful the urban jungle would swallow them and they would be forgotten: "Do not let our brethren forget to pray for us," he wrote. "Do not forget the address. It is 400 West 57th St., New York City."[8]

The year 1901 was tough in New York. The stock exchange had its first crash, and the city melted under the deadliest heat wave in its history. People jumped out of tenement windows to their deaths because the heat had become unbearable. If there was a time to leave the city and find a country cottage surrounded by green grass, leafy trees, and happy cows, this was as good a time as any. But however uncomfortable they might have been in the middle of the city, the Haskells felt called by God. They knew they couldn't just preach to people from a distance. They knew Christ's followers should follow His incarnational ministry—living and ministering *in* and *among* and *with* the urban community. Ellen White wrote to the Haskells that God "was in your going."[9]

For the Haskells, this wasn't some short-term mission trip they could finish quickly before fleeing to the safety of the countryside. This was a long-term, on-the-ground commitment. Haskell even wanted to buy a hall where "the public of this city can be reached." He hoped "that those who have means to invest in establishing a settled place for the Lord to abide in this great city will send it in."[10] While in New York, the Haskells supervised a staff of twenty people involved in Bible studies, health work, literature distribution, and much more.

I'm not leaving

In more recent years, Carl Wilkens and his wife, Teresa, and their young family were working in Rwanda—where Carl was the director of the Adventist Development and Relief Agency (ADRA). Little did they know what was about to happen. When the Rwandan genocide began, the American embassy ordered all Americans to evacuate. The Wilkenses faced a problem. Two Rwandans staying in their house—the night watchman and house girl, both Tutsi—had been specifically targeted to be killed. Carl felt compelled to stay and help them.

Despite orders from the US government and church leaders, Carl refused to leave. He and Teresa talked and prayed together and decided that she should take the children to safety, and he would stay.

Years later, I asked him about the decision. "How could I tell our Rwandan friends and coworkers that we would pray for them," he replied, "but because we had US passports, we couldn't stay with them?" Thousands left the country, and the United Nations pulled out most of its troops.

Carl was the only American who remained. Every day, he pushed his way past drunken soldiers with bloodstained clothes to deliver food, water, and medicine to orphanages. He helped save the lives of hundreds of people—including four hundred children in the Gisimba Orphanage.[11]

Mission in Liberia

Dr. Gillian Seton graduated from Loma Linda University in 2008 and then, after completing her general surgery training, went as a medical missionary to Monrovia, Liberia. Little did she know she would be thrust into a danger zone. She arrived in February 2014, just before the outbreak of Ebola, the most dreaded and deadliest virus on earth. I'd call that bad timing, but not Dr. Seton. She said that she felt like God was urging her in that direction, and "it has been the perfect fit for me."[12] "Funny as it sounds, I'm not worried," she added. "Maybe it's naïve, or fatalistic, or whatever, but if it's my time, so be it. I don't have any guarantee or conviction from God that I won't get sick. But I also know that if He still has plans for me, He'll get me through it. So, I've thought about what to do if I do start to have symptoms, but I just can't be bothered to worry about it. [I'm] too tired anyway."[13]

As the virus spread, authorities urged her to leave for the safety of the United States. But she was on a mission and couldn't be persuaded. I spoke with Dr. Seton in 2015, after Ebola. She was finally having a much-needed break at home in the United States. She told me about working seventy to eighty days in a row. The only thing that saved her from working twenty-four-hour days was a nine o'clock curfew enacted by the country's president. It meant that people couldn't get transported to the hospital until the next morning. "I knew beyond a shadow of a doubt that God wanted me in Liberia for whatever reason," she said. "He clearly led me in that direction. So that means, obviously, I was meant to be there during Ebola, and for a while now after—so we'll see what He has next."

The next year, Dr. Seton gave the commencement speech for the Loma

Linda University School of Medicine's class of 2016. "I want to help people, and I can," she said. "So, I will."

On the tightrope of mission

French acrobat Charles Blondin specialized in pushing past the comfort zones of most people. He became famous in the mid-1800s for spectacular tightrope crossings of Niagara Falls. Like the climber Alex Honnold, Blondin operated free solo, with no safety net. He argued that preparing for a disaster only made it more likely.

Stories abound of his remarkable performances on the 1,300-foot tightrope, strung 160 feet above the falls. On one occasion, he carried a small stove and utensils on his back, stopped halfway across, and made an omelet. He then proceeded to lower the freshly cooked breakfast to passengers on a boat below—adding new meaning to room service. He also made the crossing on stilts and while blindfolded. It's estimated that he made the crossing more than three hundred times.

On one occasion, Blondin reportedly transported a sack of potatoes in a wheelbarrow he pushed back and forth on the tightrope. He then bantered with the crowd, asking if they thought he could push a person to the other side in the wheelbarrow. Although the consensus seemed to be yes, strangely, he couldn't find a volunteer. He once carried his manager, Harry Colcord, across on his back. He instructed him: "Look up, Harry. . . . You are no longer Colcord, you are Blondin. Until I clear this place be a part of me, mind, body, and soul. If I sway, sway with me. Do not attempt to do any balancing yourself. If you do we will both go to our death."[14]

Stepping out of our comfort zones for Jesus isn't easy. Sometimes it can feel like walking on a tightrope over dangerous heights. And that's why Jesus' promise in the Great Commission, which we discussed in the preceding chapter, is so important: "All authority in heaven and on earth has been given to me. Therefore go . . ." (Matthew 28:18, 19).

It made all the difference for Colcord that he wasn't alone on the tightrope. He was in the control and care of the master acrobat, Blondin. And it makes all the difference when we are in the control and care of the Master—who has all authority in heaven and earth.

1. Cindy Boren, "Climber Who Fell at El Capitan Rescued With Help From Alex Honnold of 'Free Solo' Fame," *Washington Post*, November 26, 2019, https://www .washingtonpost.com/sports/2019/11/26/climber-who-pinballed-el-capitan-rescued -with-help-alex-hannold-free-solo-fame/.

2. Daniel Duane, "El Capitan, My El Capitan," *New York Times*, June 9, 2017.

3. Duane.

4. Brian Clark Howard, "Dean Potter's Extreme Life in Seven Hair-Raising Videos," *National Geographic*, May 18, 2015, https://www.nationalgeographic.com/adventure /article/150518-dean-potter-videos-wingsuit-climbing-adventure.

5. Peter L. Berger and Thomas Luckmann, *The Social Construction of Reality: A Treatise in the Sociology of Knowledge* (Great Britain: Penguin Books, 1991).

6. C. S. Lewis, *Mere Christianity* (London: HarperCollins, 2002), 131.

7. Ellen G. White, *Testimonies for the Church*, vol. 4 (Mountain View, CA: Pacific Press®, 1948), 319.

8. Stephen Haskell, "Addresses," *Advent Review and Sabbath Herald*, July 9, 1901, 14.

9. Ella M. Robinson, *S. N. Haskell: Man of Action* (Brushton, NY: Teach Services, 2004 facsimile), 194.

10. Stephen Haskell, "The Bible Training School in New York City," *Advent Review and Sabbath Herald*, November 12, 1901, 11.

11. Today Carl heads World Outside My Shoes, an organization with a goal "to equip and inspire people of all ages to build trusting relationships through restorative thinking and practices" and stand up against genocide, racism, and intolerance. "About Us," World Outside My Shoes.org, accessed February 28, 2023, https://worldoutside myshoes.org/about-us/.

12. Amy Wilkinson, "Outbreak," *Westwind: The Journal of Walla Walla University* 33, no. 3 (Fall 2014), 12.

13. Wilkinson, 13.

14. Karen Abbott, "The Daredevil of Niagara Falls," *Smithsonian Magazine*, October 18, 2011, https://www.smithsonianmag.com/history/the-daredevil-of-niagara-falls -110492884.

4

Sharing God's Mission

In a shocking decision just announced, an emergency meeting of the Executive Committee of the General Conference of Seventh-day Adventists, convening in Silver Spring, Maryland, United States, voted to cease all international mission work. "The current financial crisis has brought to a head something we've suspected for a long time," the General Conference treasurer said. "We can no longer afford to operate any kind of mission program. We need to urgently refocus our priorities and take care of our internal needs as a church."

According to the treasurer, all tithes and mission offerings will now stay in the country that collects them. This means the immediate recall of missionary medical workers, teachers, pastors, administrators, and church planters. More than a thousand international missionaries will be sent home. It also means the closing of all mission hospitals, schools, publishing houses, and media centers.

Speaking from his Silver Spring office, the treasurer argued that delegates really had no choice. "We live in uncertain economic times," he said. "Mission offerings have been declining for decades. It's impossible to fund work in new areas, and delegates felt it was time to strengthen what remains and put money into existing institutions and structures."

He urged church members to look on the positive side: "Imagine what you can do with all the money you'll now have in local churches! New furnishings, better audiovisual equipment, new Sabbath School rooms—all these should be no problem now, at least for churches in richer countries with higher standards of living. You'll now be able to keep all mission offerings and donations you were sending to Global Mission for reaching unentered areas."

"The good news is that we'll more than double the average salary of church pastors, teachers, and administrators," the president of the North American Division said. "And every local church will be able to expand its facilities, refurbish, and be more representative of our high calling as Seventh-day Adventists."

Plans are already underway for a new multimillion-dollar General Conference building in the suburbs of Washington, DC. "We've always felt a bit jealous of the Mormon temple down the road," said one General Conference departmental director, who wished to remain anonymous. "But now we'll have the money to build a better facility. Just think what a wonderful witness this new building will be to the community."

The Seventh-day Adventist Church currently has work established in 212 countries, but experts anticipate a drastic reduction after this decision. There aren't many countries where the church is truly self-sufficient. Without funding for leaders and institutions, many countries will be effectively severed from the world church. Most expect the church's worldwide membership will plummet. But at least the members who remain will worship in attractive, comfortable church buildings.

The future of the Office of Adventist Mission, which cares for church planting in unentered areas and raising mission awareness, is uncertain. There's some hope it might stay open with new terms of reference and a new name, the Office of Adventist Maintenance and Consolidation.

The director of the Ellen G. White Estate at the General Conference expressed support for the church's decision and denied it was going against the counsel of Ellen White. "It's true that Sister White said many things about the importance of supporting overseas mission," he said. "However, we must consider the wider context of the culture of the time she was writing. We must always adapt to new situations."

The Biblical Research Institute has also supported the decision of the executive committee. "We're looking closely at our traditional exegesis of Matthew 28," the director said. "It appears we may have misunderstood the original Greek and mistranslated 'into *all the world*.' Some scholars suggest that this just means *the world near you*—in other words, your local community."

While admitting the church had no other choice, the director of the Office of Archives, Statistics, and Research at the General Conference expressed sadness that the era of mission has now passed. "We'll always look back with nostalgia on those days when mission was our highest priority," he said. "In some ways, our church just won't be the same."

Disclaimer

Of course, the church wouldn't be the same. And, of course, the entire scenario I've just described isn't true. Not one word of it. Anyone I quoted, I misquoted. The idea of abandoning mission is anti-Seventh-day Adventist. But I wonder: In which direction are we headed? Does God's love still motivate us to tell the world the good news of salvation? Does it motivate us to care for the poor, the marginalized? To let people in our world know that God loves them, life has meaning, and that, one day, pain, injustice, and cruelty will end?

When we look at the line items in the budgets of our local churches, our institutions, our conferences, unions, divisions, and the General Conference, what do they reveal about our priorities? The minute we stop our financial support, our prayerful support, and our personal involvement in mission, that's the minute our church begins to die. As

Emil Brunner wrote, "The Church exists by mission, just as a fire exists by burning. Where there is no mission, there is no Church."[1]

A church faithfully holding to its mission will be a generous church, a hospitable church, a church that shares the good news of Jesus and blesses the community. When God called Abram, He called him to a special mission: "You will be a blessing. . . . All peoples on earth will be blessed through you" (Genesis 12:2, 3). The Hebrew word translated as "blessing" is *berakah*. Jong Sung Nam, a professor at World Mission University, says that *berakah* is "the ground and nucleus of Jewish liturgy" and is "the hidden soul of Jewish thought." He concludes, "We find that the berakah permeates almost every unit of Jewish worship, including the *Shema*, prayers, petitions, Scripture readings, and fellowship."[2] Nam sees this concept also playing a central role in early Christian worship; for example, in the celebration of the Lord's Supper.[3]

God calls Abram to be the conduit of God's *berakah* to "all peoples on earth" (Genesis 12:3). *Berakah* isn't just something to be received from God or given back to God but something we bestow on others. Over and over, the prophets told Israel that this was the type of worship God was calling for—action, involvement, service, and mission. Through the prophet Amos, God says He has no time for the mere accoutrements of worship—feasts, assemblies, offerings, singing—when they're separated from His mission. Instead, He says, "Let justice roll down like waters, and righteousness like an ever-flowing stream" (Amos 5:24, ESV). In place of sacrifices and burnt offerings, He wants to see mercy (Hosea 6:6), justice (Micah 6:6–8), obedience (Jeremiah 7:21–23), and care for the oppressed, the fatherless, and the widow (Isaiah 1:13–17).

Blessing all peoples

In the late 1800s, Georgia Burrus (later Burgess), a young Adventist living in California, answered this call to bless others. Perhaps the first record we have of Burrus is a note in the *Signs of the Times*® in 1888.

Each week, the paper listed donations received. Buried on page 15 of the December 21 edition is this receipt for "Foreign Missions": "Georgia Burrus $1.50." Burrus, twenty-two, was at the time a Bible worker who had become an Adventist when she was sixteen.[4] Her donation wasn't huge, but it was big enough for a young Bible worker on a low salary. It was the equivalent of about fifty-four dollars today.

Her early commitment to supporting foreign missions with her finances soon became a commitment to supporting it with her life. Burrus heard Elder Stephen Haskell describe the mission challenges of India. He made a special call for help to reach women who lived in zenanas, areas in households closed off for women only. "He told of the great need of women missionaries to work among the shut-in women of India," she later wrote. "My heart was burdened to give myself to the *Zenana* work in that needy field."[5]

At the General Conference Session held in Battle Creek in 1893, Burrus was asked to go to India and minister to these women "shut-ins." She leaped at the opportunity. To prepare, she went to Saint Helena to train as a nurse and then to a yearlong class at Battle Creek Sanitarium that trained missionaries to serve overseas. After completing her classes and after weeks of anxious waiting, news of her departure date came. A group of missionaries would soon be heading to South America, and she would travel with them as far as England.[6]

Called to India

It may seem like a stretch to compare Georgia Burrus with a biblical figure such as Abraham. They lived centuries apart, in totally different cultures. But there are echoes of his call in the life of Burrus. Abraham (then Abram) was told to leave his country and his family and go to a land God would show him. As a teenager, Burrus had become a Seventh-day Adventist despite family opposition.[7] In a way, she had already left her family. Now she was getting prepared to also leave her country. Abraham was called to be a blessing, and Georgia Burrus wanted to be a blessing in India. By faith, Burrus went as the first Adventist missionary to India.

The day finally came to catch the train to New York. From there, Burrus would travel to London and then on to India. The General Conference had already arranged for her train ticket to New York and ship passage across the Atlantic. But when it came time to head to the train station, she realized she had less than fifty cents in her purse. It wasn't enough money to get to the station. "After finishing packing my trunk," she wrote some years later, "I sat down on it to think of some way out of the difficulty."[8]

While she was sitting on the trunk, Mr. Hall, owner of the home where she was staying, burst into the room and asked why she wasn't already at the station. She told him the sorry story. He quickly exited the room and came back a few minutes later. Pressing a hundred dollars cash into her hands, he said, "May the Lord bless you and make you a blessing in India."[9] So, on Sunday, July 15, 1894, Burrus finally made it to the station and boarded the evening train for New York City. Also on the train were the families of William Thurston (who would become the first official missionary to work in Brazil) and Frank Westphal (the first ordained minister sent to Argentina).[10]

On the way to New York City, the train stopped for five minutes to let passengers view Niagara Falls. Unfortunately, fog meant they couldn't see anything. They continued, arriving in New York City the following evening. They spent one day in the city before boarding the SS *Paris* for London on the day before Burrus's twenty-eighth birthday.[11] After nearly eight days sailing, they arrived in Southampton and traveled by train to London.[12]

Burrus met up with Dores A. Robinson and his family in London. They, too, were en route to serve as missionaries in India. But she learned they planned to stay another year in England. This wasn't good news for a young woman impatient to get to her mission field. Fortunately, the General Conference gave her permission to continue alone to India and paid her fare. But this was on the understanding that once in India, she would need to support herself financially—by teaching or selling books—while learning the local language.[13]

After thirty-three days on the ship, Burrus arrived in India on January 23, 1895. She was the first single Adventist woman to venture into a non-Christian country. Burrus sailed up the Hooghly River to Kolkata (then known as Calcutta), and a launch brought mail aboard from friends on shore. Her heart sank as she wondered whether anybody would be there to meet her. But to her surprise, a man came with a letter addressed to her. It was from an older Adventist couple selling books. They had arranged for her to stay in a guesthouse. But when they went there, they discovered the accommodation had been taken by someone else.[14]

For the rest of the afternoon, they searched the city, trying to find somewhere to stay that would fit Burrus's limited budget. Finally, as the sun was setting, they found a room. But it was expensive—four rupees a day (about $1.25 back then). Burrus had only forty dollars in her purse, so she knew she couldn't stay long. The next day, she found a cheaper room at the YWCA[15]—the Young Women's Christian Association—and that turned out to be the perfect place for her to stay.

In India, Burrus threw herself into learning local languages and was soon fluent in Bengali and Hindustani. The first two baptisms in India, including the first from another religion, were the direct result of her witness. During her time in India, she worked in zenanas and set up schools and orphanages.[16] "It was not the first, nor the last, time in our work," wrote W. A. Spicer, "that a woman with the open Bible was to lead the way in a new field."[17]

Driven by faith

We're told that Abraham accepted God's call because he had faith. We aren't given any more detail than that. In the case of Georgia Burrus, we get a little more insight. She wrote, "It is the women and children of

India who call most loudly for our sympathy and help and love." Further, "What the cause of Christ needs in India above everything else is workers whose hearts are so warm and full of the love of God, and love for the souls for whom Christ died, that, in their associations with these people, they will reveal in their own lives the preciousness of the love of Christ."[18] Yes, like Abraham, she was driven by faith. But closely connected was another motivation—love.

A year after Burrus arrived in India, the Robinson family joined her. Dores Robinson was to head the work in India, based in Karmatar, Bengal. It was frontline, pioneering work, and it wasn't easy. A few years after his arrival, Robinson wrote:

> Some write and ask if it is very hot here, and say they would be glad to come and spend their lives here if it was not too warm. All we can say to such persons is that they would better not come. It *is* hot here . . . . So every one who is looking out for a nice place, free from unsightly objects,—a place with pure air, comfortable temperature, and pleasant surroundings, and where, humanly speaking, health will not be endangered,—would better not come here. But the condition that exists here is the very thing that leads us to say, "Come over, . . . and help us," and the very reason we are glad we are here.[19]

Tragically, just over a year after he wrote these words, Robinson was dead. He and another missionary, Dr. F. W. Brown, contracted smallpox and didn't recover. William Spicer, in India at the time, visited Robinson during his final days. "On receipt of word that Elder Robinson seemed bound to die, I went down and was with him in his last conscious hours," Spicer wrote. "I told him that if he must lay down his work, perhaps God would use that to draw attention to India's needs in a way that even his life might not be able to do. He replied with his swollen lips, 'Perhaps,

perhaps—I hope.' I really think his death did draw sympathy to India that counted in succeeding years."[20] Fifty-one-year-old Dores Robinson was buried in Karate, Bengal.

Three years after these deaths, seven years after arriving in India, Burrus married Luther Burgess, a fellow missionary. Later, they moved to northern India. And here is one final parallel with Abraham, who we know lived in tents (Hebrews 11:8). "Our tent is only 8 x 10," she wrote in 1907 to Elder and Mrs. Haskell, "but it is quite large enough to hold us all and all our earthly possessions, and I am sure we could not be happier if we were living in a mansion."[21]

1. Emil Brunner, *The Word and the World* (London: Student Christian Movement Press, 1931), 108.

2. Jong Sung Nam, "Roots and Tensions: Worship Patterns Developed From the Synagogue to the Jerusalem Church" (diss., Fuller Theological Seminary, 2001), 273.

3. Nam, 273–279.

4. *Seventh-day Adventist Encyclopedia*, 2nd rev. ed. (1996), s. v. "Burgess, Georgia Anna (Burrus)."

5. Georgia Burgess, "Why I Went to India," *Bible Training School*, June 1916, 5; italics in original.

6. Burgess, 5.

7. *Seventh-day Adventist Encyclopedia*, s. v. "Burgess, Georgia Anna (Burrus)."

8. Burgess, "Why I Went," 5.

9. Gordon E. Christo, "Georgia Burrus, First Adventist Missionary to India," *Southern Asia Adventist Heritage* (blog), September 10, 2015, http://sudheritage.blogspot.com/2015/09/georgia-burrus-first-adventist.html.

10. F. H. Westphal, "Journey to Buenos Ayres, Argentine Republic," *Advent Review and Sabbath Herald*, October 16, 1894, 5.

11. Obituary for Georgia Ann Burrus Burgess, "Obituaries," *Pacific Union Recorder*, October 25, 1948, 11.

12. Westphal, "Journey to Buenos Ayres," 5.

13. Burgess, "Why I Went," 6.

14. Christo, "Georgia Burrus."

15. Georgia Burgess, "My First Night in Calcutta," *Bible Training School*, July 1916, 25.

16. Georgia Burgess, "Beginning School Work in India," *Bible Training School*, November 1916, 99.

17. W. A. Spicer, "Our First Seed Sowing in India," *Advent Review and Sabbath Herald*, February 9, 1950, 1.

18. Francis M. Wilcox, "Our Work in India," *Home Missionary*, January 1897, 4.

19. D. A. Robinson, "Calcutta, India," *Advent Review and Sabbath Herald*, October 4, 1898, 10, 11.

20. W. A. Spicer, "Some Facts About Early Work in India," *Eastern Tidings*, May 8, 1941, 6.

21. Georgia Burgess, "Work in India," *Bible Training School*, February 1908, 139.

5

Excuses to Avoid Mission

A little girl was talking to her teacher about whales. She told him that in Sabbath School she heard how a big fish swallowed Jonah. Her teacher smiled at the girl's naivety. He gently explained to her that it was impossible for a big fish—even a whale—to swallow a human. A whale might be big, but its throat would be too small.

The girl wasn't convinced. She insisted that if the Bible says a big fish swallowed Jonah, then a big fish must have swallowed Jonah. Again, her teacher explained that it was a scientific impossibility. "Well," said the little girl, "I don't know how it happened, but when I get to heaven, I'll ask Jonah."

"What if Jonah isn't in heaven?" the teacher replied smugly. "What if he goes to hell?"

Without a second thought, the little girl replied, "Then you ask him."

Through the years, the story of Jonah has captured the imagination of young and old, believers and unbelievers. It has captured the imagination of painters, musicians, songwriters, and theologians. He may have been only a minor prophet, but his story has made a major impact.

Mission to an enemy city

God called Jonah to be a missionary to Nineveh, the capital of Assyria. The author of Jonah uses the literary technique of *leitwort*, deliberately repeating a specific Hebrew word for emphasis and effect. The repeated word, *yarad*, means to "go down." From the moment Jonah disobeys God, his life goes down. He goes down to Joppa, down to the ship, down into the innermost parts of the ship, and—most famously—down into the ocean and into the belly of the fish.

The Bible hints that Jonah was a country-living kind of guy. He lived in a small village called Gath Hepher, a few miles north of Nazareth—hardly a bustling metropolis (2 Kings 14:25). He lived during the rule of King Jeroboam II, when Israel was prosperous. It was a great time and place to be a prophet.

Tragically, though, along with a high standard of living came a low standard of morality. The Israelites worshiped idols, exploited the poor, and even sacrificed children. These practices enraged later prophets such as Hosea, Joel, and Amos. They thundered against broken morals and social injustice. But there's no record of Jonah ever saying a word about any of it. Apparently, he was happy sticking to his small rural parish. He even got to prophesy good news, which was a rare privilege for a Hebrew prophet (verse 25). Yes, times were good for Jonah. His name means "dove," and Jonah enjoyed his peaceful life.

But then God came and ruined everything. He gave Jonah an assignment: "Go to the great city of Nineveh and preach against it" (Jonah 1:2). How did Jonah respond to his mission call to the Assyrian capital? No doubt he looked closely at his options and reviewed recent history. He knew that a few years earlier, Assyria had brutally attacked and conquered Israel—an event that still haunted their memories. The prophet Nahum later described Nineveh as

the city of blood,
full of lies,
full of plunder,
never without victims! (Nahum 3:1).

Nahum asked a rhetorical question: "Who has not felt your endless cruelty?" (verse 19).

You can get an idea of Assyria's culture of violence from an alabaster wall relief in the British Museum in London. It's from the palace of King Ashurbanipal of Assyria and dates to the seventh century BC. The relief depicts a banquet scene with the king reclining on a couch underneath a grapevine. The queen sits on a throne across from him. On a small table near the king rest his sword, quiver, and bow—symbols of his military might. Servants fan the royal couple, while others bring refreshments and play music. Birds sing in the trees.

It's a peaceful, bucolic scene except for one thing. In the top left corner of the relief, hanging from a tree branch behind the queen is the decapitated head of Elamite king Teumman. You can easily miss the detail if you don't look closely. It's a subtle indicator of the brutal and bloodthirsty nature of Assyria. The royal couple drink their wine and enjoy the garden, totally undisturbed by the severed head decorating the tree.

Like all Israelites, Jonah knew that the Assyrians had finely nuanced ways of killing people and were experts in impaling and mutilating human bodies. It's easy to understand why Nineveh wasn't high on his list of upcoming public evangelistic meeting venues.

Jonah quickly decided he wasn't going to Nineveh. Instead, he got out his map and looked for somewhere as far away as possible. He escaped to the port of Joppa (present-day Jaffa, a suburb of Tel Aviv) and booked a Mediterranean cruise to Tarshish in Spain. This cruise was going in the direction exactly opposite the city of Nineveh. As a special bonus, it turned out this cruise included underwater sports.

Fear motivated Jonah. But it wasn't just fear that spurred his disobedience. Scholars tell us that Jonah felt a sense of cultural superiority and religious prejudice against the pagan Ninevites. But although Jonah managed to escape them temporarily, he encountered pagan sailors on the cruise ship. They asked him a series of questions that should have shaken him to the core. "What kind of work do you do? Where do you come from? What is your country? From what people are you?" (Jonah 1:8).

It's ironic that the pagan sailors got Jonah thinking about who he was supposed to be and what he was supposed to be doing. They were the voice of conscience, probing him about his identity and mission. Thousands of years later, the sailors' questions are still relevant to us. "What kind of work do you do? Where do you come from? What is your country? From what people are you?" They make us think about our identity, mission, and purpose.

A limited vision

Like Jonah, the early Seventh-day Adventist believers in the United States had a limited mission vision. They believed their mission extended from the Atlantic Ocean in the East to the Pacific Ocean in the West. They had no concept of going into all the world. They were just a "little flock" living in a big world. They saw immigrants from all over the world flooding into American cities. They reasoned, conveniently, that they could fulfill the gospel commission without leaving the shores of America.

Adventist historian Arthur Spalding says that this was a "comforting rationalization."[1] W. A. Spicer suggested that the little flock would have been discouraged if, at first, they had grasped a proper understanding of their mission. "The work had to grow," he wrote, "and with it the comprehension of the believers."[2] It wasn't until the late 1860s that they started to realize they had a mission to foreign lands.

On April 1, 1874, Ellen White had a dream in which she heard a messenger say, "You are entertaining too limited ideas of the work for this time. You are trying to plan the work so that you can embrace it in your arms. You must take broader views. Your light must not be put under a bushel or under a bed, but on a candlestick, that it may give light to all that are in the house. Your house is the world."[3]

Hundreds of years earlier, God gave Israel the same message. He told them their vision was too small:

> It is too small a thing for you to be my servant
> > to restore the tribes of Jacob
> > and bring back those of Israel I have kept.
> I will also make you a light for the Gentiles,
> > that my salvation may reach to the ends of the earth (Isaiah 49:6).

A few chapters later, He again calls for a larger vision: "And my blessings are for Gentiles, too, when they accept the Lord; don't let them think that I make them second-class citizens" (Isaiah 56:3, TLB).

What does this larger vision look like in practice? Let's look at another prophecy. Isaiah writes, "On that day there will be a highway from Egypt to Assyria, and the Assyrian will come into Egypt, and the Egyptian into Assyria, and the Egyptians will worship with the Assyrians. On that day Israel will be the third party with Egypt and Assyria, a blessing in the midst of the earth" (Isaiah 19:23, 24, NRSV). These are astonishing words—the pagan nations of Egypt and Assyria worshiping God along with Israel?

Yes, indeed. In fact, there's more: "There will be an altar to the Lord in the midst of the land of Egypt" (Isaiah 19:19, ESV). This must have shocked Jewish ears. An altar in Egypt? They knew all about idolatrous Egypt and its superstitious practices, full of magic rituals and the worship of animals. And yet here is God saying that His vision—His larger vision—was to see an altar to Him established in the heart of that pagan country.

The lesson Jonah needed to learn, the lesson Israel needed to learn, the lesson the early Adventist movement had to learn, and the lesson you and I and our church today need to learn is that God has an unlimited vision for mission. There's a wideness in God's mercy.

On a boat toward their mission

In the previous chapter, we saw how Georgia Burrus sailed to London on the SS *Paris* with two other missionary families. After she stopped in London, the Thurstons and Westphals continued to South America. Their boat stopped at Rio de Janeiro, where the Thurston family disembarked. Frank Westphal and his wife, Mary, both in their thirties, and their son and baby daughter continued to Argentina. They arrived on August 18, 1895.

Within a week, Westphal was on a boat heading up the Paraná River. His destination was a Russian-German village where he'd heard there were Adventist believers. While on the boat, in freezing weather, he caught a bad cold. When the boat arrived, he had to ride thirty miles on a horse to Diamante, where the Sabbath keepers lived.

A farmer invited him to stay in his adobe house. Placing a coat on the dirt floor, he handed Westphal an old blanket for a covering. Westphal lay down that night on the floor among the farm fowl. But within minutes, lice and fleas attacked him. He headed outside to escape the pests, but the neighborhood dogs put a quick end to that. He ended up spending the night standing in the kitchen.[4] In his understated report in the *Advent Review and Sabbath Herald*, Westphal remarked, "The welcome morning finally came, and I was glad."[5] Despite the warm welcome from the local wildlife, Westphal remained in that village for three weeks, studying with the people every night. Within two weeks, he had organized a church of thirty-six members—the first Seventh-day Adventist church in South America.[6]

In his first thirteen months in Argentina, Westphal was home for barely six weeks. Later, during a five-month trip to Brazil, he baptized William Stein, the first Adventist convert there. He returned home, exhausted. Sadly, tragedy met him.

"When I arrived . . . home, my wife and . . . son met me at the door," he wrote, "but my little daughter Helen did not appear. There was scarcely need to ask what had happened. The mother's griefworn face told me."[7] Baby Helen, eighteen months old, had contracted measles and then scarlet fever in his absence. Mary had buried their daughter two weeks earlier in Chacarita Cemetery in Buenos Aires. She had gone through the unthinkable ordeal without her husband by her side. "She longed for someone near and dear to share her grief," he wrote, "and yet none was near nor even knew of her loss."[8] A missionary from another denomination had conducted the funeral ceremony.

If ever there was a time to pack up their bags and go home, surely this was it. This wasn't an excuse to leave the mission field; it was a compelling reason to leave. But somehow, Frank and Mary continued, opening new work all over Argentina and in neighboring Uruguay. Finally, they returned home on medical leave in 1901. After three years, they went back to South America for another seventeen years of service.

Modern-day Joppas

Today, like Jonah, we stand in our own Joppas. Which direction will we go? Our calls may be vastly different from what Georgia Burrus and the Westphals received. But where are our Ninevehs? As we look at the growth of today's Ninevehs, God's rhetorical question at the close of the book of Jonah echoes down the centuries to us: "Should I not have concern for the great city of Nineveh?" (Jonah 4:11). Should I not be concerned about Lagos and Los Angeles; about Dhaka and Delhi; about Sydney and São Paulo; about London and Lahore?

What excuses keep us from engaging in mission today? Is our vision big enough to shed tears for children growing up with no meaning and no hope? Does our vision extend to the 10/40 Window, where 65 percent of the world's population lives and only 15 percent of Adventists live? Does it extend to the state of Uttar Pradesh in India? If this one state were a country, it would be the fifth largest country in the world. We have one Adventist church for every two million people in that state. Is Uttar Pradesh a Nineveh about which we should be concerned?

Studies suggest that we're not concerned. In fact, researchers estimate that 91 percent of all Christian resources—financial means, human power, projects, and programs—go toward Christians. Less than 10 percent is directed toward the vast numbers of non-Christians.

Simon Bar Jonah

Jonah stood in Joppa. Hundreds of years later, so did the apostle Peter, whom Jesus called Simon Bar-Jonah (Matthew 16:17, ESV). God had a larger vision for Jonah and called him to go to the Gentiles. God also had a bigger vision for Peter and the early church, and He called Peter to go to the Gentiles.

God called Jonah to Nineveh and Peter to Caesarea. Jonah protested by instead going on his Mediterranean cruise. Peter protested in words: "Surely not, Lord!" (Acts 10:14).

God intervened in Jonah's plans through a storm and a fish. He intervened in Peter's plans through the vision of unclean food. God gave both Jonah and Peter the same instructions: "Arise" and "go" (Jonah 1:2; Acts 10:20, NKJV). Finally, in both cases, the Gentiles believed and were forgiven. Sadly, in both cases, there were hostile reactions to these conversions. In Jonah's case, he got angry. In Peter's case, the hostile reaction came not from him but from the "circumcision party" (Acts 11:2, 3, ESV).

God rebutted Jonah at the conclusion of that magnificent book with the words, "Should I not be concerned about Nineveh, that great city . . . ?" (Jonah 4:11, NRSV). And He rebutted the circumcised skeptics by giving the Gentiles the same spiritual gift they themselves had received.[9]

Today, we stand in Joppa. Are we headed for Nineveh? Are we headed for Caesarea? Or are we enjoying a Christian Mediterranean cruise?

---

1. Arthur Spalding, *Origin and History of Seventh-day Adventists*, vol. 2 (Washington DC: Review and Herald®, 1962), 193.

2. William A. Spicer, *Our Story of Missions for Colleges and Academies* (Mountain View, CA: Pacific Press®, 1921), 90.

3. Ellen G. White, *Christian Experience and Teachings of Ellen G. White* (Mountain View, CA: Pacific Press®, 1922), 216.

4. Floyd Greenleaf, *A Land of Hope: The Growth of the Seventh-day Adventist Church in South America* (Rodovia: Casa Publicadora Brasileira, 2011), 37.

5. F. H. Westphal, "Argentine Republic," *Advent Review and Sabbath Herald*, October 30, 1894, 6.

6. Greenleaf, *A Land of Hope*, 37, 38.

7. Greenleaf, 141.

8. Greenleaf, 141.

9. These comparisons come from Robert W. Wall, "Peter, 'Son' of Jonah: The Conversion of Cornelius in the Context of Canon," *Journal for the Study of the New Testament* 9, no. 29 (1987): 80.

6

Motivation and Preparation for Mission

It was April 1916. The reality of millions dying in what became known as the Great War was largely unknown to Americans. The longest battle of World War I, the Battle of Verdun, raged on the other side of the Atlantic. For now, America was at peace and still a year from declaring war on Germany.

A few years earlier, thousands of Japanese cherry trees of various types were planted around the Tidal Basin in the nation's capital, Washington, DC. The result was a spectacular burst of color every spring. And in the spring of 1916, love was in the air for John Andrews and Dorothy Spicer, two young Seventh-day Adventists living there.

John was completing his training at the medical school of George Washington University in downtown Washington, DC. (Coincidentally, at the same time, in the university's law school, a young J. Edgar Hoover, later to be the powerful and controversial first head of the FBI, was completing his studies.) "Ever since our second year we have been the proud possessor of John," stated the 1916 university yearbook. "Prior to that, he was an asset to the College of Medical Evangelists. He intends to attend the New York Post-Graduate Medical School and later go to China as a medical missionary."[1]

John's girlfriend, Dorothy, was a nursing student at Washington Sanitarium. It was in nearby Takoma Park, home to the new headquarters of the General Conference of Seventh-day Adventists and associated institutions. Dorothy was born in India, where her parents—William and Georgia Spicer—served as missionaries from 1898 to 1901. During those three years, their lives of service interlinked with that of Georgia Burrus, whom we met in the previous chapter.[2]

In 1901, Dorothy's father became secretary of the General Conference Mission Board, and two years later, he was elected secretary of the General Conference of Seventh-day Adventists. He worked closely with General Conference president A. G. Daniells. Under their leadership, the Adventist Church enjoyed what would become known as a golden era of Adventist missions, where missionaries went all over the globe. Spicer later served as General Conference president from 1922 to 1930.[3]

Dorothy inherited her parents' mission impulse. When her family arrived in Takoma Park from India in 1904, she attended fourth grade at a nearby public school. No doubt, her teacher, Mrs. Cora Taltamus, was surprised when her young student invited her to Sabbath School. But she accepted the invitation, became a Sabbath School member, and was later baptized.[4]

If mission ran through her veins, Dorothy met a good match in John Andrews, who also came from strong missionary stock. His grandfather, J. N. Andrews, after whom he was named, was the first official overseas missionary sent by the Seventh-day Adventist Church.[5]

A hidden marriage

In 1916, society frowned on young people getting married while still in college. Many parents aren't keen on it even today. But John and Dorothy hatched a plan. One afternoon, they dropped Dorothy's mother, Georgia, at a concert she wished to attend in Washington, DC. While Dorothy's mother, blissfully unaware, enjoyed the music, the couple drove north to Baltimore to complete their clandestine mission. Fortunately for them, the road between DC and Baltimore had been completely paved the year before, making their journey a little quicker.[6]

In Baltimore, they found a minister to marry them. There was no formal church service. No family. No friends. Just a minister and the daring offspring of two great Adventist missionary families. Immediately after the ceremony was performed, the new husband and wife drove back, picked up Mrs. Spicer, and told her the news. We're left to imagine her reaction, but we know she was sworn to secrecy. A few weeks later, they shared the news at a graduation party for Dorothy's younger sister. The party doubled as a reception for the wedding nobody had attended.[7]

If a taste for adventure and an ability to push the envelope are qualifications for successful missionaries, John and Dorothy were probably overqualified. Within weeks of graduating and getting married, they joined a large group of missionaries headed for China. In fact, it was the largest group of missionaries sent anywhere at one time by the Seventh-day Adventist Church. It was also reportedly the largest group ever sent by any denomination to China. More than forty missionaries, plus children, left San Francisco on August 1 on the steamship named, appropriately, SS *China*. The steamship was literally a slow boat to China, with stops in Honolulu, Yokohama, Kobe, and Nagasaki en route to Shanghai.[8] An article in the *Pacific Recorder* compared the sailing of John Andrews with the sailing of his pioneering grandfather forty-two years earlier: "A splendid band of recruits are following in his footsteps by leaving their homes and going out to the ends of the earth in search of the lost."[9]

For the newlyweds, that boat was the only place for them to be. "For one brought up in a home such as mine, the natural consequence was to prepare for, and expect to go to a mission field," Dorothy wrote. "So with my husband. To go out and work for ourselves, for our own advancement, simply never occurred to us. Therefore, it was not surprising that six weeks after my doctor's graduation, we were leaving for China. China—of all the places which did not appeal to me at all!"[10] Here was the motivation for their mission. They simply assumed that they would live for others, not for themselves.

A slow boat to China

Despite the war and the uncertain international political climate, it was a heady time for Adventist mission. Writing in the third quarter *Mission Quarterly* in 1916, W. T. Knox reported that the General Conference Annual Council the year before was "deluged with requests from our brethren in foreign fields." He added, "Never in any previous council have such large demands been made upon the denomination from mission fields."[11] More than one hundred missionary families required transportation to their posts of duty in 1916. The third quarter of that year had fourteen Sabbaths instead of thirteen, so the Fourteenth Sabbath Offering was designated for "landing the 1916 recruits."[12]

After arriving in Shanghai, the Andrewses traveled to Chungking, Southwest China, where the Yangtze and Jialing Rivers merge. It was a thirteen-hundred-mile trip inland by boat, foot, and a sedan chair. This strategically located port city had opened to foreigners and trade in 1890. The Andrewses served there for more than two years, but their hearts were set on going to the mission frontier of Tibet.[13] On June 10, 1919, they set off on a long, difficult, and dangerous trip to Tatsienlu (modern-day Kanding) on the Tibetan border. John Andrews had conducted an exploratory trip with fellow missionary Merritt Warren the previous year. During that journey, robbers shot at them, and authorities detained them several times.[14]

It took nearly two months for Dorothy, John, and their baby son, Robert, to travel by boat up the Yangtze River. At one stage, within seven miles of their final port, their boat was wrecked. All their belongings—including food, clothes, and books—were thoroughly drenched.[15]

Back on the road, Dorothy recalls riding, baby in her lap, in a sedan chair carried on poles by Chinese laborers.[16] She felt embarrassed having men carry her and would often leave the chair to walk.[17] Sixty-nine laborers carried the missionaries' goods, and twelve soldiers escorted them.[18] "Steamer trunks which are too heavy," recalled Dorothy, "must be tied between *two* long bamboo poles and carried by *two* men who can manage a hundred and fifty pounds between them."[19] There were other indignities and difficulties on the way, such as eyes peeking through cracks in the wall of their bedroom and the sounds of animals being slaughtered in the room next door.[20] Dorothy also lamented, "Baby has reached the word-learning stage, and has acquired some unspeakable swear words from the chair men."[21]

Life in Tatsienlu

The Andrews family soon settled into life in Tatsienlu. John opened a clinic, and they established a mission compound. Medical work opened doors throughout their stay. As Dorothy put it, "A medical missionary in China possesses a master key to the hearts and homes of every class of people."[22] Medical work connected them to the community. "The interest of the Chinese and the Tibetans in the gospel is very slight," wrote John.[23] But he added, "Our dispensary work has brought us into friendly and favorable touch with many people."[24] He visited many monasteries where Tibetan Buddhist monks lived. "[They] soon became friendly," he said, "on learning that we could help their sores and aches and pains."[25]

He found the Tibetan people physically brave. A middle-aged woman with fluid accumulated in her abdomen came to see him. John saw scars from previous procedures. She told him that in the past, the fluid had been drained by piercing her abdomen with a hot iron tube. "She was pleased to find our methods less heroic," he said.[26]

Tatsienlu was a major hub for the tea trade. Through acquaintances made with traders who came to the clinic, John sent gospel tracts in

Tibetan back across the border into Lhasa and other places, sewn up in packages of tea.[27]

The Andrews's five children were born in China. Tragically, during their first furlough home in 1923, their five-month-old baby, Judy, died of whooping cough. It was a terrible irony to have survived all the hardships and dangers of service in China only to lose their beloved baby back home in Takoma Park. Despite the tragedy, the family returned to the front lines of mission in Tatsienlu the following year.[28]

In Tatsienlu, sentiment against foreigners started to grow until, in 1926, the Andrews family had to flee for safety. It was the middle of winter, and they traveled over treacherous mountain passes to Chentu. From there, they headed to Chungking by bamboo raft and boat. They arrived in the middle of the night, and across the river, they could see the city on fire. They found refuge in the American consulate until they found passage on a steamer to Shanghai. There they remained until 1928, when the family undertook another perilous journey back to Tatsienlu. They continued serving there until 1932, when they felt it was time to return home to America.[29]

Mission adventure

Dorothy and John had gone to China in 1916 as a young couple on a mission adventure. They found it. They did have missionary DNA in their blood, and a life given to service wasn't so much expected as just taken for granted. But undergirding it all it was the motivation of love—love for Jesus and love for the people of China. Dorothy wrote:

We go to help them because we love Jesus. Arriving, we find folk, very different from our own countrymen, and not, to our prejudiced mind, so lovable. But we work and pray and hope all things for them. We laugh with them in their joys and comfort them in their sorrow and minister to them in their sickness, and out of it all there is born a love that is much like the love of a mother for her child. It is that feeling that calls the missionary back to lonely, uncomfortable places even before his furlough is over, and enables him to disregard difficulties as mere incidentals.[30]

Fittingly, Dorothy was echoing the thoughts of her father, who wrote some years earlier, "May every heart that knows the forgiving grace of Jesus be ready to say with Isaiah, 'Here am I; send me.' Isa. 6:8."[31]

---

1. *The Cherry Tree*, yearbook, George Washington University (1916), 111.

2. Jonathan Gomide, "Andrews, John Nevins (1891–1980) and Dorothy Josephine Spicer (1892–1979)," *Encyclopedia of Seventh-Day Adventists*, May 12, 2022, https://encyclopedia.adventist.org/article?id=6HSB&highlight=dorothy|spicer.

3. "Register of the William A. Spicer Papers," collection 3, Adventist Heritage Center, Andrews University, accessed March 7, 2023, https://www.centerforadventist research.org/wp-content/uploads/collections/C0003%20-%20William%20A.%20 Spicer%20Papers.pdf.

4. " 'Little People' and Sabbath School Evangelism," Potomac, *Columbia Union Visitor*, December 28, 1967, 8.

5. In 1874, J. N. Andrews and his two children, Mary, sixteen, and Charles (who would become John's father), seventeen, went to Switzerland as missionaries.

6. "John and Dorothy Andrews," The Andrews Family: Adventism's First Family of Missions—Virtual Exhibit, Center for Adventist Research, Andrews University, accessed March 6, 2023, https://www.centerforadventistresearch.org/andrews-family -exhibit/10/#john-and-dorothy.

7. "John and Dorothy Andrews."

8. wanderernolonger, "Travels in China—The Overseas Chinese," Past Presence, November 6, 2019, https://past-presence.com/2019/11/06/travels-in-china-part-2-the -overseas-chinese/.

9. T. E. Bowen, "Among Our Missionaries," *Pacific Union Recorder*, December 14, 1916, 2.

10. Dorothy Spicer Andrews, "Missionary Memories," *Youth's Instructor*, August 21, 1934, 5.

11. W. T. Knox, "The Problem of the Treasury," *Missions Quarterly* 5, no. 3 (Third Quarter 1916): 4, 5.

12. Knox, 6; W. A. Spicer, "The Official Notice," *Missions Quarterly* 5, no. 3 (Third Quarter 1916): 4.

13. "Tibet (Western China)," The Andrews Family: Adventism's First Family of Missions—Virtual Exhibit, Center for Adventist Research, Andrews University, accessed March 9, 2023, https://www.centerforadventistresearch.org/andrews-family-exhibit/14/.

14. "Itinerating in West China," Division Notes, *Asiatic Division Outlook*, May 15 and June 1, 1918, 15.

15. J. N. Andrews, "In the Gateway to Tibet," *Advent Review and Sabbath Herald*, December 18, 1919, 19.

16. Dorothy Spicer Andrews, "Missionary Memories: On the Trail," *Youth's Instructor*, September 25, 1934, 13.

17. Dorothy Spicer Andrews, "Missionary Memories: Still Traveling West," *Youth's Instructor*, October 2, 1934, 9.

18. C. C. Crisler, "Our Tibetan Mission: A Challenge," *Advent Review and Sabbath Herald*, March 19, 1936, 10.

19. Andrews, "On the Trail," 7; italics in original.

20. Andrews, "Still Traveling West," 13.

21. Dorothy Spicer Andrews, "Missionary Memories: Home at Last," *Youth's Instructor*, October 16, 1934, 8.

22. Dorothy Spicer Andrews, "Missionary Memories: Just Living in Tatsienlu," *Youth's Instructor*, November 6, 1934, 14.

23. J. N. Andrews, "Pioneer Work in Tatsienlu," *Asiatic Division Outlook*, January 1, 1922, 3.

24. Andrews, 3.

25. J. N. Andrews, "Work in Eastern Tibet," *Advent Review and Sabbath Herald*, August 19, 1926, 9.

26. Crisler, "Our Tibetan Mission," 10.

27. Florence Nagel, "John Nevins Andrews MD," Chinese SDA History, accessed March 14, 2023, https://www.chinesesdahistory.org/john-nevins-andrews-m-d?rq=Andrews.

28. "John and Dorothy Andrews and Their Family," The Andrews Family: Adventism's First Family of Missions—Virtual Exhibit, Center for Adventist Research, Andrews University, accessed March 13, 2023, https://www.centerforadventistresearch.org/andrews-family-exhibit/13/.

29. Nagel, "John Nevins Andrews MD"; Wilma Warren, "Pressing on Toward Tatsienlu," *Far Eastern Division Outlook*, July 1928, 10.

30. Dorothy Spicer Andrews, "Missionary Memories: Off for Tibet," *Youth's Instructor*, September 11, 1934, 7.

31. William A. Spicer, *Our Story of Missions for Colleges and Academies* (Mountain View, CA: Pacific Press®, 1921), 12.

7

Mission to My Neighbor

The sacrifice and commitment of missionaries such as Dorothy and John Andrews may sound like a foreign concept to many in today's "selfie" generation. The word *selfie*—referring to pictures you take of yourself—sadly entered our vocabulary in 2002. An Australian posted the first known use of the word on September 13 on an online forum. "Um, drunk at a mates [sic] 21st, I tripped ofer [sic] and landed lip first (with front teeth coming a very close second) on a set of steps. I had a hole about 1cm long, right through my bottom lip. And sorry about the focus, it was a selfie."[1]

It was an undignified start to the word, but eleven years later, *selfie* was named the *Oxford English Dictionary*'s word of the year. The dictionary's publisher noted that usage of the word had increased by 17,000 percent during the previous year.

In recent years, selfie museums have started all over the world. The Original Selfie Museum has locations in eight places in North America at the time of this writing. It claims that it's "the first creative space uniquely designed to take your Photos and Videos to an entirely new level of Awesomeness."[2] These installations feature a variety of different backdrops and contexts, all designed for one thing—to inspire you to take more pictures of yourself.

In the beginning God

There are good reasons the Bible doesn't begin with the words "In the beginning, I" or "In the beginning, we." Right from the start, God's Word directs us away from ourselves to God—"In the beginning God" (Genesis 1:1). Everything begins with God.

When humans are created on the sixth day, the emphasis is still on God:

Then God said, "Let us make man in our image. . . ."

So God created mankind in his own image,
in the image of God he created him;
male and female he created them (Genesis 1:26, 27).

God didn't create Adam and Eve in the same way He created on previous days. He created them according to the divine blueprint. As Ellen White writes: "Every human being, created in the image of God, is endowed with a power akin to that of the Creator—individuality, power to think and to do."[3]

God created human beings in community—"It is not good for the man to be alone" (Genesis 2:18). People who reflect the image of God care for others, not just themselves. Jesus connected love for God with love for our neighbor (Matthew 22:37–39). The first recorded betrayal of the image of God after the Garden of Eden is the murder of Abel. When God questioned Cain about his brother, he showed no remorse: "I don't know," he replied, "Am I my brother's keeper?" (Genesis 4:9).

Human history follows two themes that emerge from being created in God's image. The first is how we've strayed from that image, and the second is how God has been working to restore that image.

In today's disoriented world, instead of looking up, we're looking down. Instead of worshiping the Creator, we're worshiping the created. God created us to worship Him, and we're more interested in selfies. In today's selfie world, it's almost impossible to see a picture of the Eiffel Tower or the pyramids or the White House without someone's beaming face decorating the foreground. It reminds me of the cartoon that said, "It's too bad your selfie stick isn't long enough to capture how ridiculous you look using a selfie stick." Perhaps that's a little unkind.

In a *New York Magazine* cover article in 1976, novelist Tom Wolfe declared the 1970s "The 'ME' decade." Nearly four decades later, a *Time* magazine cover read, "The Me Me Me Generation: Millennials are lazy, entitled narcissists who still live with their parents."[4] The truth is, every generation since the beginning of time has been a me generation. To some extent, every generation has taken its eyes off God and focused on itself.

But while we've been focusing on ourselves and obscuring the image of God, He's been working to restore that image in us. And He calls His church to join Him in that task. As Ellen White wrote, "The true object of education is to restore the image of God in the soul."[5] We're called to act like people created in God's image. That means joining God's mission to restore His image in creation. Among other things, people reflecting God's image will reflect His love and kindness to their neighbors. They'll treat them with dignity and respect. They'll work for justice and show compassion for the poor and marginalized. They won't need to ask the question, "Am I my brother's keeper?" They'll know the answer.

Amoeba and human

Consider the difference between a human being and a one-cell amoeba. The most obvious difference is that the amoeba has one cell while a human has at least thirty-seven trillion (plus a few million microbes).

Admittedly, a one-cell amoeba has a degree of cleverness. It can move.

It can alter its shape. It doesn't have a mouth, but it can ingest food. It can even reproduce. Sadly, some of us have moved so far from the image of God that we function almost at the level of an amoeba. We move, alter our shape, ingest food, and reproduce. And that's about it.

It reminds me of graffiti I saw some years ago: "Live. Consume. Die." That sums up life for many of us today. A one-cell amoeba lacks creativity. It couldn't compose Handel's *Messiah* if it tried. It couldn't write a Shakespearean sonnet. It couldn't paint the *Mona Lisa*. But then again, it wasn't made in the image of God.

You don't ask an amoeba to be its brother's keeper. You don't ask if it's making moral choices, being fair and just, or reflecting the image of God. You don't expect an amoeba to be a good Samaritan. But we do expect these things from human beings, who, unique among creation, are made in God's image. We should also expect these things from His church, which has the mission of working to restore the image of God in humanity.

How are we reflecting the image of God?

In 2015, the Pew Research Center reported that the Seventh-day Adventist Church is the most racially and ethnically diverse religious group in the United States. That's wonderful news for a church that has accepted the commission to go into all the world and make disciples of all people—a church that believes all people are created in the image of God and all people are equal, a church that appreciates the strengths coming from different languages, cultures, and peoples. It's good for a church that appreciates the strengths coming from different languages, cultures, and peoples.

Some years ago, writer A. J. Jacobs said, "I got an email from a man in Israel who had read one of my books, and the email said, 'You don't know me, but I'm your 12th cousin. . . . I have a family tree with 80,000 people on it, including you, Karl Marx, and several European aristocrats.' "[6]

Jacobs was fascinated. "*This is remarkable,*" he thought. "*Here I am alone in my office, but I'm not alone at all. I'm connected to 80,000 people around the world.*"[7] That message inspired him to start working on his family tree. At last count, he was up to 92 million people. Jacobs proudly declared he was related to President Obama—"he is my aunt's fifth great-aunt's husband's father's wife's seventh great-nephew, so practically my old brother."[6]

Of course, human connectivity shouldn't surprise us. As the apostle Paul wrote many years ago: "And he made from one every nation of men to live on all the face of the earth, having determined allotted periods and the boundaries of their habitation" (Acts 17:26, RSV). God told Abraham that he would be the father of all nations (Genesis 12:1–3). That means that you and I are all brothers and sisters, cousins, aunts and uncles, nephews and nieces. And the church is a family of disciples that brings together a complex, multicolored, multitextured, multigifted network of cultures, backgrounds, and spiritual gifts to the glory of God.

In the church, "there is neither Jew nor Greek, there is neither slave nor free, there is neither male nor female; for you are all one in Christ Jesus" (Galatians 3:28, NKJV). Barriers and prejudices we might expect in other social groups shouldn't be seen in the body of Christ. Differences that might divide others give us strength. That strength enables us to show compassion and care for our neighbors, no matter their race, gender, politics, age, religion, or lack of religion.

Breaking down barriers

Scan through the second chapter of Paul's letter to the Ephesians, and you'll see how sin separates us from God and from one another: "You were separate from Christ, excluded from citizenship . . . and foreigners . . . , without hope and without God" (verse 12). "You . . . once were far away" (verse 13). But Jesus breaks down barriers, and so we see Him reconciling (verse 16), being "our peace," and destroying "the barrier, the dividing wall of hostility" (verse 14).

Many scholars believe that this "dividing wall" is a specific historical reference to a wall in the Jewish temple. In Isaiah, God says, "My house shall be called a house of prayer for all peoples" (Isaiah 56:7, ESV). The temple had a specific court where Gentiles could visit. But there was one section where they couldn't enter, the section that contained the Most Holy Place.

In 1871, French archaeologist Charles Simon Clermont-Ganneau found a stone from Herod's temple with an inscription that warned Gentiles not to enter this forbidden section. Today you can view that stone in the Istanbul Archaeology Museums. The penalty for disobeying the warning was death. Although addressed specifically to the Gentiles, the warning also applied to Jews. The issue wasn't so much whether you were Jew or Gentile; it was whether you were ritually impure. Jews didn't need a warning sign; they knew the rules.

Paul uses a Greek word in Ephesians 2:14, *mesotoichon*, which is translated as "the dividing wall of hostility" (RSV) or "middle wall of partition" (KJV). The problem is that it doesn't appear anywhere else in the Bible, so nobody knows for sure what Paul had in mind. Even if he wasn't referring specifically to the temple wall, it's still a powerful image of Jesus knocking down walls that separate and exclude.

Speaking of exclusion, I'm an Australian citizen, and I have a green card that permits me to work in the United States. I carry it wherever I go, and it's not a good idea to lose it—particularly when returning to America from overseas. My current one isn't so bad, but the first card the United States government kindly issued had a photo of me looking like a criminal. At the top were the words "Resident Alien." It even assigned me a resident alien number. The wonderful thing is that in the Christian community, nobody is a resident alien. Jesus has broken down the walls: "So then you are no longer foreigners and strangers" (Ephesians 2:19).

From east and west and north and south

At the great wedding feast of the Lamb, described in Revelation, who will be sitting at the table? A select few from a select race of people? No! "People will come from east and west and north and south, and will take their places at the feast in the kingdom of God" (Luke 13:29).

In the church at Antioch, God began to build that multicultural fellowship. Here, for the first time, Jewish and Gentile Christians worshiped God together on equal footing (Acts 11:19–26). We also see a diverse leadership team. Barnabas was from Cyprus (Acts 4:36). Simeon was probably a black African convert. Lucius of Cyrene was possibly from North Africa, and Manaen was probably a wealthy Greek-speaking Jew. Saul, of course, was a Jew born in Tarsus and a Roman citizen. Under this team, the Antioch church grew until it replaced Jerusalem as the mother church. Soon the Antioch church became a missionary church, sending church planters across the then-known world.

The Holy Spirit directed this movement of Jesus' followers, who came to believe that all people were created in the image of God. This movement worked to restore that image in Jews, Greeks, Romans, and pagans. They treated people with love, dignity, and respect. As sociologist Rodney Stark says, "The Christians introduced into a world of hatred and cruelty a totally new concept about humanity—that you had a responsibility to be compassionate and caring to everyone."[7]

Stark points out that when Greeks left newborns on the hillsides to die, Christians cared for and nursed these babies who had been cast aside. When pagan priests fled plague-ridden cities for the safety of the countryside, Christians remained to care for the poor and the sick. And it was Christians who elevated women from being mere possessions. Why did the early church grow so rapidly? Because Christians treated their neighbors as people made in the image of God. It grew rapidly because Christians loved God with all their hearts and loved their neighbors as themselves.

1. N. "Hopey" Hope, "re: Dissolvable Stitches," ABC Online Forum, September 13, 2002, quoted in Matt Liddy, "This Photo, Posted on ABC Online, Is the World's First Known 'Selfie,' " ABC News, November 18, 2013, https://www.abc.net .au/news/2013-11-19/this-photo-is-worlds-first-selfie/5102568.

2. Original Selfie Museum, accessed March 14, 2023, https://originalselfiemuseum .com/.

3. Ellen G. White, *Education* (Mountain View, CA: Pacific Press®, 1952), 17.

4. *Time*, May 20, 2013, https://content.time.com/time/magazine/0,9263,7601 130520,00.html. Millennials are people born between 1981 and 1996.

5. Ellen G. White, *Patriarchs and Prophets* (Mountain View, CA: Pacific Press®, 1958), 595.

6. A. J. Jacobs, "The World's Largest Family Reunion . . . We're All Invited," TED, accessed February 13, 2023, https://www.ted.com/talks/a_j_jacobs_the_world_s_largest _family_reunion_we_re_all_invited.

7. Jacobs.

8. Paul Galloway, "How Jesus Won the West," *Chicago Tribune*, March 27, 1997.

8

Mission to the Needy

Some years ago, a group of Australian teenagers was surveyed to find the name of the most recognized sports star. Was it the captain of the Australian cricket team? Of the rugby league team? Perhaps one of Australia's gold medal–winning swimmers? No to all the above. It was American basketballer Michael Jordan.

Around the same time, many Australian teenagers started wearing baseball caps backward. That makes sense in the hot Australian sun, protecting the back of your neck from harmful rays. But that wasn't why they were doing it. Reportedly, the backward cap–wearing phenomenon first started in America because of a Sylvester Stallone movie in 1987. Such is the power of a movie star. Soon other actors and hip-hop music icons continued the trend, which skyrocketed in the 1990s when star baseballer Ken Griffey Jr. wore his cap that way. Teens in America soon started emulating these stars, and the reversed-cap movement drifted across the Pacific Ocean to Australian teens.

The attraction of a Big Mac

The first McDonald's restaurant in Moscow, Russia, opened on January

31, 1990. It was the world's largest McDonald's, built for more than fifteen thousand customers a day. Thousands of Muscovites lined up in freezing temperatures waiting for the doors of the restaurant to open. Was it because McDonald's offered superior cuisine? At the risk of offending some readers, not exactly. Burgers and fries may have been a novelty, but it wasn't exactly fine dining. Was it because the food was cheap? Not at all. For an average worker in Russia, McDonald's was wildly expensive. The *New York Times* reported on a factory worker who, for example, spent "four days' salary on a Big Mac, cheeseburger, apple pie and two milkshakes."[1]

Nobody forced those first-day diners to hand over hard-earned rubles. No military herded them into line. They went to McDonald's because they wanted to. They lined up because the golden arches—which meant burgers, fries, shakes, packets of ketchup, and smiling uniformed servers—stood as a metaphor for the West, freedom, and the American way of life. For Russians moving out of Communism, that's exactly what they wanted to taste. This was yet another step in what has been termed the Coca-Colonization[2] of the globe, a phenomenon in which American popular culture reaches around the world, from Mexican farmers drinking Coca-Cola to African villagers watching Seinfeld reruns to Japanese teens listening to Taylor Swift.

Culture is power

The global influence of American culture is an example of what has been called "soft power." In the late 1980s, political scientist Joseph S. Nye Jr. wrote a groundbreaking work entitled *Soft Power: The Means to Success in World Politics*. Naturally, when we think of global power, we think about having the best weapons, the strongest military, and the ability to dictate terms around the world. Nye calls that "hard power." But just as important, he argues, is something he calls "soft power." This is something a nation has that attracts people and makes them want to emulate and follow it. It doesn't require tanks.

Like it or not, the United States' formidable military commands respect around the world. But its soft power also circles the globe—through things such as sports, fashion, fast food, Hollywood movies, and popular music. A country isn't powerful only because it has big guns; it's powerful because it attracts people. When its influence holds sway around the globe.

Today there are organizations that specialize in ranking the soft power of countries. As of this writing, for example, the Global Soft Power Index ranks the United States as number one, followed in order by the United Kingdom, Germany, China, and Japan. It's China's best performance ever in the index rankings. One major reason, according to the Global Soft Power Index, is that it has done well in the "generous" metric. During the COVID-19 pandemic, for example, it offered many countries free protective equipment and vaccinations. That's soft power in action.[3]

According to this index, Australia was ranked in the top ten countries for a year. That's when other countries watched enviously as it appeared to expertly manage COVID-19 and keep infection rates low. But that perception changed "as the nation sealed itself off from the rest of the world." David Haigh, chairman and CEO of Brand Finance, called it "their COVID-induced retreat from the interconnectedness of the modern world."[4]

For many years, South Korea has taken the concept of soft power seriously. In her 2013 inauguration speech, South Korean president Park Geun-hye stated, "In the 21st century, culture is power."[5] Over the past several years, Hallyu—also known as the Korean Wave, the rise in popularity of Korean TV programs, computer games, and K-pop—has taken the world by storm. People from Brazil to India to Iran watch Korean soap operas. Teenagers in Africa, Asia, and the Americas listen to K-pop stars. Gamers all over the world play Korean computer games.[6]

This isn't an accident; it didn't just happen. Over the past few decades, the Korean government has intentionally invested billions of dollars into cultural exports. The Korea Trade-Investment Promotion Agency has 127 Global Offices in 86 countries, and they closely measure the reach of the Korean Wave in major countries around the world.[7]

Why has South Korea invested so much in its cultural industries? It knows that soft power attracts international goodwill, and goodwill attracts investment. The popularity of K-pop and soap operas sells records, merchandise, and advertising. They inspire people to buy Korean cosmetic products, clothing, and food. They enrich the Korean economy.

Jesus' soft power

What does all this have to do with mission? The bottom line is that the gospel is shared most effectively through spiritual soft power. Soft power most effectively reaches the marginalized and those whom Jesus saw as "harassed and helpless, like sheep without a shepherd" (Matthew 9:36). It also best touches the lives of those who feel they are "rich, and increased with goods, and have need of nothing" (Revelation 3:17, KJV).

The most effective soft power comes through direct human contact. We see this most clearly through the example of Jesus. Ellen White says His ministry had five key components:

1. He mingled among people "as one who desired their good."
2. He showed people sympathy.
3. He ministered to people's needs.
4. He won people's confidence.
5. He bid people to follow Him.[8]

This can't be done from a distance. She goes on to say, "There is need of coming close to the people by personal effort. If less time were given to sermonizing, and more time were spent in personal ministry, greater results would be seen. The poor are to be relieved, the sick cared for, the sorrowing and the bereaved comforted, the ignorant instructed, the inexperienced counseled. We are to weep with those that weep, and rejoice with those that rejoice. Accompanied by the power of persuasion, the power of prayer, the power of the love of God, this work will not, cannot, be without fruit."[9]

There's nothing pushy or manipulative about Jesus' method of ministry. He knocks at the doors of our hearts. He doesn't try to knock them down. This isn't to say that hard power doesn't have its place in mission. Apologetics, for example, uses logic, argument, and evidence to defend the Christian faith. It appeals to reason, data, and scholarship. It aims to persuade the mind. The apostle Paul used this method when he reasoned with people in the marketplace, quoted pagan literature to pagans, and philosophized on Mars Hill (Acts 17). Adventists use it in seminars, public meetings, and evangelistic literature. But hard power has its limitations: "While logic may fail to move, and argument be powerless to convince, the love of Christ, revealed in personal ministry, may soften the stony heart, so that the seed of truth can take root."[10]

Spiritual soft power is all about connection. It engages and influences communities. It's like a spiritual breeze that isn't trapped within the four walls of a church building. It touches people's hearts as well as their heads. It's an influence that comes through people—people who leave the church pews to connect with the community. It comes through Jesus' followers who are putting His method of mission into practice.

Soft-power connections

"How Trump Won: Now He Just Needs the Votes" declared *Time* magazine's cover on January 18, 2016. This was well before Donald Trump became the forty-fifth president of the United States in November of that year. Reading the article, I came across the word *disintermediation*.[11] I'd never seen the word before and discovered it refers to getting rid of the middleman. In this article, David Von Drehle showed how Trump broke with the normal ways of communicating with the American public. Rather than relying on journalists to deliver his message, he went directly to the people. He did that mainly through mass rallies and social media, particularly Twitter. He didn't filter his thoughts through traditional media gatekeepers, through middlemen. Like it or not, it worked.

In recent decades we've seen other examples of disintermediation. I can't remember the last time I used a travel agent. It's far quicker and more efficient for me to book plane tickets and hotels directly, usually through the internet. Disintermediation made Amazon founder and CEO Jeff Bezos the richest man in the world. Rather than going physically to a store to buy a book, you can pay Amazon to deliver it directly to your door. In America, it can arrive within a day or two. But if you have a Kindle reading device, you can download the book digitally almost anywhere in a matter of seconds. Meanwhile, thousands of physical bookstores have gone out of business.

Not so long ago, people would drive to a video store to rent a video to take home to watch. In the United States, Blockbuster Video stores were a billion-dollar enterprise. Today people download thousands of movies and TV programs directly to their electronic devices without stepping outside their houses. Blockbuster Video and thousands of other video stores collapsed almost overnight.

Martin Luther, in the sixteenth century, was one of the earliest examples of disintermediation. He taught that we can directly approach God without the need for an intermediary priest. In other words, we don't need a religious go-between. Today, there are other religious "go-betweens" that are problematic. A few years ago, an Adventist organization in the United States sent out a fundraising email for their literature ministry. "Greetings!" it said. "Hit the streets with soul-saving literature without leaving the comfort of your own home!" In other words, the church member is a "middleman" who's not needed. All you have to do is send your money, put up your feet, have a long cool drink, and let the ministry do the rest.

No shortcuts

There should be no disintermediation in mission. There are no good shortcuts in mission. Every Jesus follower is called to be personally involved. And yet the temptation is to outsource it to literature, television, radio, or the internet. Or to bring in an evangelistic "professional" who can run public meetings for your local church, which requires little ongoing commitment of time or resources by church members.

Of course, all these things can be wonderful tools for sharing the good news. Many people have come to faith in Jesus Christ and joined the Seventh-day Adventist Church through various media. But these tools can only support and never replace personal involvement. And candidly, the number of people who read, watch, or listen themselves into the church is relatively few. The majority of Seventh-day Adventists still join the church because of the direct soft-power influence of Seventh-day Adventist Church members.

The Incarnation

Jesus demonstrated the ultimate rejection of "mission from a distance." The apostle John calls Him the Logos (John 1:1). The Jewish understanding of the *logos* directly connects it to God as the Creator and to His teachings, or the law (Deuteronomy 32:45–47). Greeks used the word differently. For them, it was a life force infusing the world and keeping everything in balance. The *logos* was reflected in the symmetry of a leaf, the harmony of the seasons, and the order of the stars in the sky. For both his Jewish and Greek readers, John makes a startling claim: this *logos* became flesh and broke into human history in the form of a specific person in a specific place at a specific time with a specific purpose. As John writes,

"And the Word [*logos*] became flesh and dwelt among us, full of grace and truth" (John 1:14, RSV).

God wasn't content to present the *logos* as an abstract philosophical or theological concept floating around in books and poetry and song. He put skin and bones on it in the form of a baby born in a real town, in a real country, at a real point of time in history. And this is the model for effective witness today: Jesus followers mixing and mingling with people, rubbing shoulders with them in the street, bumping into them in the neighborhood grocery store, and talking to them over the fence.

I playfully tell church planters that the best way to make connections in the community is to have a baby. When you're out walking the baby in the evening, everybody wants to stop to admire him or her. Everybody finds babies adorable—I guarantee no neighbor will ever say, "What an ugly baby!" (at least not directly to you). And if you're lucky, you'll run into other parents out with their babies. The baby provides a springboard for communication with anyone. It provides moments of shared humanity with strangers.

If, for whatever reason, it's not practical or possible to have a baby, the second-best option is to get a dog. Make sure it's fluffy, cute, and doesn't bark at strangers. Then when you're out for a walk, you'll meet other people walking their dogs. You get to talk about your canines, compare notes, and make a connection. The only danger is that you'll get to know the names of all the dogs in the neighborhood and not their owners'!

All of this is slightly tongue-in-cheek, but it serves a point. Direct human connection is the key to effective mission. When Fernando and Ana Stahl went as missionaries to the Peruvian Andes in 1909, they began using the time-honored Adventist technique of selling literature. The problem was that political and religious elites were oppressing the impoverished population, and 95 percent of them were illiterate. The Stahls adapted and refocused their ministry into a creative, wholistic approach—starting schools, clinics, markets, and, unwittingly, a social revolution.[12]

Educator and congressman José Antonio Encinas visited the town of Plateria and saw what they were doing. He wrote: "The basic thing is that they [the Adventists] are transforming the spirit of the Indian, bringing him into civic life, making him aware of his rights and obligations, separating him from the vices of coca and alcohol, removing superstition, curing illnesses, showing the best way toward human dignity."[13] Their soft-power mission transformed the lives of the helpless and the most vulnerable. It brought hope and healing. It was spiritual soft power in action.

1. Francis Clines, "Moscow McDonald's Opens: Milkshakes and Human Kindness," *New York Times*, February 1, 1990.

2. Mark Pendergrast, "A Brief History of Coca-Colonization," View Points, *New York Times*, August 15, 1993.

3. "Global Soft Power Index 2022: USA Bounces Back Better to Top of Nation Brand Ranking," Brand Finance, March 15, 2022, https://brandfinance.com/press -releases/global-soft-power-index-2022-usa-bounces-back-better-to-top-of-nation -brand-ranking.

4. *Global Soft Power Index 2022* (London: Brand Finance, 2022), https://brandirectory -live-public.s3.eu-west-2.amazonaws.com/reports_free/brand-finance-soft-power -index-2022.pdf.

5. 윤민식, "The Full Text of Park's Inaugural Speech," *Korea Herald*, February 25, 2013, https://www.koreaherald.com/view.php?ud=20130225000590.

6. Bernadine Racoma, "Hallyu or Korean Wave Continues to Take the World by Storm," *Day Translations* (blog), July 30, 2018, https://www.daytranslations.com/blog /korean-takes-world/; Sophy Topley, "Seoul Sister: How Korean Culture Has Taken the World by Storm," Tatler, October 13, 2022, https://www.tatler.com/article/korean -wave-k-pop-south-korea-culture-popularity.

7. "KOTRA's Regional Support Centers," Location Report, Invest Korea, May 9, 2018, https://www.investkorea.org/ik-en/bbs/i-2486/detail.do?ntt_sn=475733.

8. Ellen G. White, *The Ministry of Healing* (Mountain View, CA: Pacific Press®, 1942), 143.

9. Ellen G. White, *Gospel Workers* (Washington, DC: Review and Herald®, 1915), 363.

10. White, 185.

11. David Von Drehle, "Donald Trump's Art of the Steal," *Time*, January 16, 2017, https://time.com/4170772/the-art-of-the-steal/.

12. See Charles Teel Jr., "Mission Stories and the Adventist Future: Fernando and Ana Stahl as a Case Study," *Adventist Education* 55, no. 2 (December 1990/January 1991): 16–19, 45, 46.

13. J. Samuel Escobar, "Religion and Social Change at the Grass Roots in Latin America," *Annals of the American Academy of Political and Social Science* 554, no. 1 (November 1997): 100.

9

Mission to the Powerful

In chapter 2, we saw how Judas's death left just eleven disciples. Soon after Jesus left for heaven, those remaining disciples gathered to discuss their future. What were they to do? How would they do it? What should be their first move? Now that Jesus was gone, how should they go about building His church?

They got down to business immediately. Their priority was to elect a president to lead their new movement. They clearly needed an exceptional leader with a strong vision and proven experience in building a team. But most important, they needed someone who could effectively connect with the rich and powerful. They desperately needed credibility and influence. And that required a highly respected leader who could get the new movement officially registered by the government.

The challenge facing them was all too clear as they looked around the room and the handful of believers. Nobody was qualified. Most came from humble backgrounds, and few had graduated from high school. None had influential, powerful contacts.

Finally, by a slim majority, they voted for Peter. Everyone knew he wasn't a great candidate, although nobody said it publicly. It was no secret that he had denied Jesus just before His crucifixion. They also knew he was a mere fisherman. But they had to have someone.

Next, they needed a marketing director. To start a strong movement, they desperately needed funds for resources, to pay missionaries, to build churches, to run children's and youth ministries, and to fund literature. And how could they launch a public relations campaign without money? The list of needs was long. Unanimously, they chose Joseph of Arimathea. Joseph, or Joe to his friends, was wealthy and knew business inside and out. Now that Judas was gone, he was the only person they knew who had any knowledge of the subject.

They also needed to build team unity. While Jesus was with them, He kept things together. He knew exactly how to manage their backbiting and ambition. But now that He was gone, some of the old wounds had opened again, and there was bickering.

Fortunately, Nicodemus had good contacts in the business world who owed him a favor, and they organized some team-building exercises. The consultants took the disciples through different scenarios. One went like this: "Imagine you're holding a convention with several thousand people attending. It comes time for lunch, and you discover someone forgot to organize catering. What would you do? In the next hour, work together and come up with a plan." Another scenario was: "Imagine your leader gets arrested for something he didn't do. You then learn that he's had a sham trial and has been sentenced to death. Put together a plan to save him."

At the end of the day, the disciples finished up, frustrated and discouraged. They failed every scenario. They just couldn't seem to see eye to eye on anything, let alone work together to solve a problem.

A friend of a friend of one of the disciples knew an author who had been on the *Jerusalem Times* Best-Seller Scroll list for the past six months. The scroll was entitled *How to Start a Movement in Ten Easy Steps*. She came and gave them an inspiring seminar. She clearly outlined the key elements needed in any successful movement: a likable, charismatic leader; a strong vision; an effective public relations team; and significant funding. But at the end of her presentation, the disciples again went home discouraged. They had none of the things necessary to start a movement.

They also urgently needed a strategic plan. Joe Arimathea brought in some specialists from the business school at the elite Jerusalem School of Management. The professors started with constructing a vision statement. Philip, one of the more thoughtful disciples, quietly suggested they could use Jesus' parting words, "Go ye into all the world . . ." The consultants thought he was joking and started laughing. But by the look on his face, they saw he was serious. Surprised at his naivety, they gently suggested that a group of eleven penniless, powerless, uneducated followers of a former traveling Rabbi should start with something a little less ambitious than going into all the world!

After the consultation, the professors returned to the Jerusalem School of Management feeling embarrassed for these followers of Jesus. They'd just been doing a favor for their friend and colleague Joseph, but they knew the reality. There was no way in the world this undisciplined group of uneducated former fishermen and assorted uneducated hangers-on would be able to achieve anything. Into all the world, indeed! Perhaps they might be able to rally a handful of recruits among a village or two in Galilee. People who didn't know anything better. But reaching anybody of importance or influence? Starting a movement? Laughable!

Of course, we know that's not what happened. The book of Acts tells a very different story. But at the time, anyone looking on must have wondered how a small, motley crew of spiritually weak Jesus followers would continue His mission on Earth. One thing is for sure: the young Christian movement wouldn't move forward by human cleverness and smart marketing techniques. It wouldn't grow through pandering to the powerful. It wouldn't flourish through strategies proposed by the Jerusalem School of Management. Certainly, Jesus wanted them to use the best methodologies and be well educated in how to reach the various people groups they would meet. But only the Holy Spirit could make them effective.

Improvising the witness

King Frederick the Great of Prussia once played a trick on the great composer and musician Johann Sebastian Bach. He told his court musicians to come up with a tune that would be difficult to turn into a fugue (a musical composition with several interweaving melodies). But when they gave the tune to Bach, he didn't hesitate. Sitting at the keyboard, he improvised on the spot, effortlessly composing a fugue with three different intertwining melodies. He shocked the king and his musicians. Then, a few weeks later, Bach sent the king a written-out fugue on the same tune, but now in six parts. Six separate and distinct melodies blending together, and all based on one notoriously difficult tune. Some experts say this was the greatest musical achievement of all time.

In some ways, pure improvisation is a myth. It doesn't happen out of nothing. Bach was certainly a genius. But he could be a master improviser only because he was also a consummate musician with an intricate knowledge of how music works and is put together.

You must be well prepared to improvise well. Sir Winston Churchill was famous for his quick wit and spontaneous speeches. But there was some truth to the joking comment of his best friend, F. E. Smith: "Winston has spent the best years of his life composing his impromptu speeches."[1]

That's why Jesus' first instruction was for the disciples to do absolutely nothing. They weren't to start a public evangelistic series for the Jerusalem elite. They weren't to start planting churches in Judea. They weren't to start distributing truth-filled literature in Caesarea. He instructed them simply to wait—"But stay in the city until you have been clothed with power from on high" (Luke 24:49).

They needed time for prayer, fellowship, and study of Scripture. They needed to wait for power from the Holy Spirit. He would lead them to improvise their lives and witness in a totally new situation—an unprecedented situation—right there on the edges of the Roman Empire. He would empower them for the most important mission ever entrusted to anyone in the history of the world, an assignment given to a group of broken men who, a few days earlier, had denied their Lord.

Under the power of the Holy Spirit, the church became agile, nimble, and ready to improvise. The book of Acts is the remarkable story of how the Holy Spirit took a handful of unlikely candidates and shaped them into the pioneers of the mightiest movement this world has ever seen. Under the power of the Holy Spirit, we see all sorts of methods and models of outreach used. Under the power of the Holy Spirit, we see signs and wonders performed. The church became one, with the believers sharing with one another (Acts 4:32). It enjoyed the favor of the people and grew (Acts 2:47).

In 2020, the COVID-19 pandemic pushed the world into uncharted waters and forced the church—you and me—to improvise. People who thought church was a building where you meet once a week had to rethink their assumptions. Ministries had to face ministering with fewer funds. Organizations had to restructure for greater efficiency. And the ability of any group or person to adapt depended, to a large extent, on how well prepared they were before the pandemic hit.

Mission to the powerful

The book of Acts tells how churches were soon being planted all over the Roman Empire. Christianity spread among the Jews and the Gentiles, young and old, men and women. It certainly spread among the poor, but sociologist Rodney Stark refutes the prevalent idea that it was just a movement of the lower classes. "From the very beginning," he writes, "Christianity was especially attractive to people of privilege."[2]

Stark points to rich men connected to Jesus, such as Zacchaeus (Luke 19:1–10), Jairus (Luke 8:40–56), and Joseph of Arimathea (Matthew 27:57). There were also women, such as Joanna, wife of Herod's steward, and Susanna—both wealthy women who supported Jesus (Luke 8:3).[3] This trend continued in the early church after Jesus departed. Stark details how the apostle Paul "attracted many privileged followers." He quotes Gillian Cloke: "[Early Christianity] had substantial purchase amongst the classes of those capable of being patronesses to the apostles and their successors."[4] Some might point to Paul's first letter to the Corinthians, where he says that not many of them were "powerful" or "of noble birth" (1 Corinthians 1:26, ESV). But Stark argues, "Given what a miniscule [*sic*] fraction of persons in the Roman Empire were of noble birth, it is quite remarkable that *any* of the tiny group of early Christians were of the nobility."[5]

Continuing His mission

Jesus' departure to heaven left His eleven disciples bereft. No longer would they have their Mentor, Teacher, and Guide physically beside them. There they were, a ragtag crew of bickering disciples who, a few days earlier, were ready to deny their Lord. Now they were given the most important assignment and the most important mission ever entrusted to anyone.

But He didn't leave them alone. The book of Acts tells the remarkable story of how the Holy Spirit took these unlikely candidates and shaped them into bold pioneers of a missionary movement. A movement that had a life-changing message of hope and healing for all people, including those who are rich and increased with goods and feel as if they need nothing.

---

1. Nicholas Soames, "Sweat and Tears Made Winston Churchill's Name," *Telegraph*, May 4, 2011, posted on International Churchill Society, https://winstonchurchill.org/resources/in-the-media/churchill-in-the-news/sweat-and-tears-made-winston-churchills-name/.

2. Rodney Stark, "Christianity: Opiate of the Privileged?" *Faith and Economics* 54 (Fall 2009): 2, http://christianeconomists.org/wp-content/uploads/2020/05/2009-Fall-Stark.pdf.

3. Stark, 5.

4. Stark, 6; Gillian Cloke, "Women, Worship, and Mission," in *The Early Christian World*, ed. Philip F. Esler (London: Routledge, 2000), 427, quoted in Stark, 6.

5. Stark, 2.

10

Mission to the Unreached: Part 1

"Woe to you, scribes and Pharisees, hypocrites!" said Jesus. "For you cross sea and land to make a single convert, and you make the new convert twice as much a child of hell as yourselves" (Matthew 23:15, NRSV). Those sound like terrible words for Jesus to say. But He was just warming up. He went on to also call them "blind fools" (verse 17), "blind guides" (verse 16), "snakes" (verse 33), and "a brood of vipers" (verse 33). If that wasn't enough, they were also "like whitewashed tombs, which on the outside look beautiful, but inside they are full of the bones of the dead and of all kinds of filth" (verse 27, NRSV). And then, in case someone still didn't get the point, they were also "full of hypocrisy and lawlessness" (verse 28, NRSV).

For Jesus, the problem wasn't so much what the religious elite taught. In fact, He told the crowds to follow their teachings (verse 3). The problem was their behavior: "They do not practice what they teach" (verse 3, NRSV). How had these highly regarded, highly ethical religious scholars and leaders come to such a place? And what lessons do we, as Adventists, need to learn? We're also in the business of crossing land and sea, endeavoring to faithfully follow the Great Commission. Do we share any of the guilt of these leaders?

Scholars disagree about what Jesus meant by scribes and Pharisees crossing sea and land to make converts. There's little hint of such a thing elsewhere in the New Testament apart from, perhaps, the apostle Paul as a Jewish follower of Jesus. There's certainly no strong evidence of Pharisees officially going as missionaries to the Gentiles. Some believe Jesus is referring to Pharisees persuading other Jews to follow Pharisaic *halakha*—their interpretation of the law and how people should live. Whatever the meaning, Jesus describes a process through which the scribes and Pharisees are making new converts "twice as much a child of hell" (verse 15).

Acting badly for Jesus

Since Jesus' time, there's been no shortage of people who've acted badly in the name of Christian mission. In the Middle Ages, armed Christian crusaders marched into battle with flags bearing the symbol of the cross. In the sixteenth century, Spanish conquistadors forced indigenous Mexicans to become Christians by the force of the sword. Portuguese explorer Ferdinand Magellan "converted" as many as possible to the Catholic faith while on his remarkable sea voyage from Europe to Asia. In 1521, while in what's known today as the Philippines, he converted more than two thousand local people.

Magellan heard that chieftains on a nearby island, Mactan, were refusing to convert. He sent a message that if they didn't comply, he would confiscate their property and execute them. Not exactly an inspirational altar call. The islanders may not have understood the Western concept of confiscating property, but they did understand execution. Still, they chose to ignore the threat.

In response, Magellan sent some of his men to the island to set a village on fire. This motivated many to convert, but they still kept their idols and sacrificed to them. One holdout was Lapu, a chieftain from the village that Magellan's men had razed to the ground. In an unholy alliance of missionary zeal and colonialism, Magellan sent him a message saying that if he would "obey the king of Spain, recognize the Christian king as their sovereign, and pay us our tribute, he would be their friend; but that if they wished otherwise, they should wait to see how our lances wounded."

Lapu declined the kind invitation, and Magellan linked forces with the chief of the island, Sula, to attack. But as the story goes, Lapu's men greatly outnumbered Magellan's men. As they fell at his side, Magellan himself was struck in the right leg with a poisoned arrow. This was followed with more blows—a bamboo spear to his arm, a cut to the leg from a large cutlass. And there, helpless, he fell faceward in death.[1]

Message. Method. Motivation.

We naturally read with horror stories such as this. In our mission to the unreached, our message matters. But methods and motivations are just as important.

Best-selling travel writer and novelist Paul Theroux describes paddling his kayak among the Trobriand Islands of Papua New Guinea. He came across a Seventh-day Adventist village. "What distracted my attention was the good health of the villagers, in particular their good teeth," he writes. One of the villagers invited him to stay in their village. I love the conversation Theroux recalls:

> "The missionary will show you a place."
> "Where is the missionary?"
> I expected to see a *dim-dim* [white man] in a black frock, but instead I was greeted by a Trobriander in a T-shirt and bathing suit.
> "I am the missionary," he said.[2]

Theroux, a religious cynic, later listened to John (the missionary) give his testimony.

"I was blind. I spent many years as a blind man," he said. "Then I became a Seventh Day Adventist [*sic*] and I learned to see. Paul, would you like to learn how to see, like your namesake on the road to Damascus?"

So, they were Seventh Day Adventists: that obviously explained their good teeth. They did not smoke or drink, the younger ones did not chew betel. No pig-eating.

"Do you want to convert me?"

"Yes. I do."

"I'll have to think it over, John. It's a pretty big decision in any person's life."[3]

I'd be honored to meet that young Papua New Guinean missionary dressed in a T-shirt and bathing suit. I love how he spoke naturally and directly and shared his testimony honestly and openly. He had no idea their conversation would end up in a best-selling book read by tens of thousands of people. Of course, this is just Theroux's version of the encounter. And he wasn't converted. But it was through no fault of that young Adventist man of faith. There was something so genuine about his witness that Theroux, a world-weary cynic, didn't belittle him in any way.

How we say things is almost as important as what we say. Sometimes religious language can get complicated and confusing. Of course, religion doesn't have a monopoly on that. Recently, I was copied on an email that included these two sentences: "One potential solution by implementing entities is a manual adjustment at year-end to 'transfer' the unspent balance of the trust fund through revenue to an allocated fund. A reversing entry could be made at the beginning of the new fiscal year to put the funds back into a trust fund, if that is desired."

This might be perfectly understandable to an auditor or accountant, but to my untrained eye, it's a foreign language. I have no idea what it means. "Manual adjustments," "reversing entries," and "allocated funds" belong to a different universe from mine.

The nice thing, though, is that I don't have to understand these things. Let the finance people care for them. Let them use their jargon. That's why they went to business school. If that language helps them work more effectively and efficiently, so be it. No harm done.

Jargon becomes a problem only when we're trying to communicate something important to people outside our group. Like when we're sharing the good news. And that's something that we, as Seventh-day Adventists, should treat seriously. Take, for example, one of our fundamental beliefs, number 26, "Death and Resurrection," which says, "The wages of sin is death. But God, who alone is immortal, will grant eternal life to His redeemed. Until that day death is an unconscious state for all people. When Christ, who is our life, appears, the resurrected righteous and the living righteous will be glorified and caught up to meet their Lord. The second resurrection, the resurrection of the unrighteous, will take place a thousand years later."[4]

This statement expresses beautiful truth. It makes perfect sense to most Adventists. But people without a Christian background would struggle to understand it. And most of the world doesn't come from a Christian background. When sharing this fundamental belief with a nonbeliever, we need to translate it—just like from one language to another. A key part of effectively reaching the "unreached" is finding tools that will help us connect with people who look at things differently than we do. Tools that will help us share the truths of God's Word attractively and meaningfully, being sensitive and alert to different cultural understandings.

The doctrine of salvation

Take the doctrine of salvation. The Bible uses many different word pictures to help us understand it. Here are just a few: adoption (Romans 8:15), redemption (1 Peter 1:18, 19), reconciliation (Romans 5:10), justification (Galatians 2:16), liberation (Romans 6:18), marriage (Romans

7:2–4), inheritance (Romans 8:17), forgiveness (Luke 1:76, 77), and being found (Luke 15:31, 32). These word pictures open different windows on the idea of salvation, helping us better understand what Jesus has done for us. They reveal different insights, different angles, on something we won't fully understand until we get to the kingdom.

Someone might ask, "Which metaphor is correct?" Well, they're all correct! They all point to the beauty of what God has done for us. But if we focus only on one, we lose the richness provided by the others. Paul's legal metaphors of redemption and justification had particular resonance for people steeped in the Roman system of law. Jesus' story of the prodigal son is powerful across cultures, including non-Christian ones. Virtually everyone knows how it feels to be lost.

Our challenge, if we're to reach "the unreached," is to share the good news in ways that are understandable, meaningful, and attractive. Simply handing a copy of the 28 fundamental beliefs to a Kalahari bushman or a Silicon Valley computer programmer or a Wall Street banker isn't going to cut it. If we follow the example of Jesus and the apostle Paul, we'll prayerfully try to share the message in a way that connects with them. And that will look different according to the audience. That doesn't mean compromising or watering down the truth or encouraging syncretism. The truth of salvation doesn't change, but the way we communicate it does. The apostle Paul knew that he needed to adapt his message to different audiences. Or as Ellen White put it, "[Paul] varied his manner of labour, shaping his message to the circumstances under which he was placed."[5]

Stop. Look. Listen.

One of the most important but often forgotten steps in mission work is to first stop and listen. It's a lesson Kasim Reed learned in the summer of 2009. Reed, a forty-year-old attorney, was campaigning to become mayor of Atlanta, Georgia. It wasn't going well. "You're super-losing," a friend told him.

Reed's political consultants told him that he needed to be out on the streets meeting more people. So, there he was, in the heat of an Atlanta summer, knocking on a door in Mechanicsville, one of the city's oldest neighborhoods. "Hello, I'm Kasim Reed," he said, using the opening lines he'd rehearsed at other houses. "I'm a Georgia state senator, and I'd like to be your mayor. May I talk to you about the campaign?" An old woman "with a warm face" looked through her steel-barred door and invited him inside. Pouring him a cool drink, she invited him to sit. "Tell me why you think you should be mayor," she said.

Reed delivered his spiel: Atlanta is the cradle of the civil rights movement; it has a large concentration of Fortune 500 businesses; it operates the world's busiest passenger airport; it boasts wonderful restaurants. "And I believe I can make the city stronger," he finished. "She looked at me as if I were a Martian," recalls Reed. "None of this was getting through. I felt terrible."

The woman took Reed outside and said, "Let me show you the Atlanta I know." There was an empty swimming pool with boys shooting dice. To the left stood a gazebo that was now covered in gang graffiti. Young men were playing loud music.

"That's the Atlanta that I know, baby," she said. "Let me tell you something else. I'm a pretty good cook myself, so I don't go to the restaurants you're talking about. And if I was going to go to restaurants, I'd need to take the bus, and I don't really feel safe going out at night right now. And that airport that you all are always talking about, baby, I don't fly. Now you have a nice day."

Reed left that house discouraged. The plan was to visit 150 houses a day with no more than three minutes spent at each. He'd spent fifteen valuable minutes with this old woman, and he was convinced she didn't like him and wouldn't vote for him. But that fifteen minutes proved invaluable for the future mayor of Atlanta. "I changed that day," he says, "because what I understood from that visit with Miss Davis was that until you see a city how people who are most in need of help see it, you're never going to reach them. And I was never the same."[6]

Too often, Christians try to sell airports to people who don't fly. That's why you can't just dream up a mission strategy in a denominational boardroom. Broad principles can be agreed on, but application in every situation differs. We need to spend time listening to the Miss Davises of this world. We need to talk to community leaders, business leaders, shopkeepers, teachers, doctors, and neighbors. We need to look carefully at local newspapers and online community forums. What are people talking about? What makes them happy? What keeps them awake at night? We can't even begin to communicate with people until we know where they're coming from and what their needs are.

In mingling with people on dusty roads, in cities and villages, in homes, and on hillsides, Jesus saw firsthand and close-up their needs. He saw tears running down their cheeks. He saw questions in their eyes. And He shaped His messages in ways that connected. But most important, Jesus bathed His ministry in love. Matthew tells us that when Jesus "saw the crowds, he had compassion on them, because they were . . . like sheep without a shepherd" (Matthew 9:36). This kind of compassion must be the purpose and foundation of all our mission activities.

When we put Christ's method of ministry into practice, our brothers and sisters from different faiths and those with no faith soon learn that we love and care for them. And when we accidentally say the wrong thing or make a cultural mistake, they're usually quick to overlook it.

But that doesn't excuse us from doing all we can to understand people's faiths and cultural contexts. As Jesus instructed His first missionaries: Be "wise as serpents, and harmless as doves" (Matthew 10:16, KJV), especially when crossing land and sea as missionaries.

1. This story comes from Laurence Bergreen, *Over the Edge of the World: Magellan's Terrifying Circumnavigation of the Globe* (London: HarperCollins, 2009).

2. Paul Theroux, *The Happy Isles of Oceania: Paddling the Pacific* (New York: Ballantine Books, 1993), 116, 117.

3. Theroux, 117, 118.

4. "Belief 26: Death and Resurrection," Seventh-day Adventist Church, accessed February 15, 2023, https://www.adventist.org/death-and-resurrection/.

5. Ellen G. White, *Gospel Workers* (Washington, DC: Review and Herald®, 1915), 118.

6. TEDPrizeChannel, "TEDCity2.0: Kasim Reed," YouTube video, October 20, 2014, https://www.youtube.com/watch?v=semT61CCNEE.

11

Mission to the Unreached: Part 2

The Babylonian exile totally upended the lives and understanding of thousands of Jewish people. King Nebuchadnezzar's armies had ruthlessly torn the exiles from their homes, culture, and people. The first wave of the Jewish exile, in 605 BC, occurred during the reign of King Jehoiakim of Judah. Nebuchadnezzar besieged Jerusalem and pillaged it, including its sacred temple. He herded Jews like cattle back to the pagan city of Babylon. Among those exiles were four young men: Daniel, Shadrach, Meshach, and Abednego.

Wrenched away from all that was familiar, they were left with virtually no spiritual support system. We don't know whether they even had any written Scripture. Perhaps they could only cling to passages they'd memorized during family worship. What did the four young captives think about during that long and cruel deportation? The grief of their parents? Their mothers' home-cooked meals? Their comfortable beds?

It's some five hundred miles as the crow flies between the cities of Jerusalem and Babylon. But to avoid the harsh desert, the Babylonians probably took the exiles on a much longer, more circuitous route. They weren't flying on Babylonian Airlines with first-class seats and kosher meals. They were taken and transported as slaves.

Babylon the Great

Archaeology gives us insights into what it must have been like for those exiles arriving in Babylon. Between 1899 and 1917, Robert Koldewey and Walter Andrae excavated thousands of bricks and fragments of the Ishtar Gate and shipped them to Berlin. Today, in the Pergamon Museum in Berlin, you can see a reconstruction of that gate with its magnificent blue and yellow glazed bricks depicting ornate lions, dragons, and goddesses. Imagine the impression it made on Daniel and his friends as they passed through this majestic walled entrance into Babylon.

After entering the city, they would have proceeded down Processional Way, paved with large stones, connecting to the temple of Marduk, the chief deity of the city. On the way, they would pass palaces, more temples, and other magnificent buildings. In every direction they turned, more splendor dazzled their eyes.

And yet, the reality of daily life in this pagan city would soon hit home. This was no short-term mission trip, a temporary diversion before returning to the comforts of home. For all they knew, it was permanent banishment to a pagan city with foreign customs, foreign languages, foreign food, and foreign gods.

For Daniel and his three young friends, religion wasn't some sort of optional extra, a part-time hobby, something to dabble in once a week. Judaism was their way of life. It structured their lives, their days, and their seasons. It dictated their behavior. But in Babylon, their religion was considered nothing. Most people in Babylon had never even heard of Yahweh.

The university of Babylon

Daniel and his friends attended the university of Babylon, where they learned "the language and literature of the Babylonians" (Daniel 1:4). For the first time, they studied a worldview totally opposed to their Jewish tradition. The Babylonians didn't worship Yahweh, they didn't keep Jewish dietary laws, and they'd never heard of the Ten Commandments.

Archaeological discoveries suggest what the curriculum for "wise men" at this time would have looked like. It probably included pagan creation and flood stories, the Akkadian language, and divination texts. They would have learned how to tell the future by watching the stars, pouring oil into water, and reading omens from sheep livers. We glimpse this pagan worldview in Ezekiel's description: "For the king of Babylon stands at the parting of the way, at the head of the two ways, to use divination. He shakes the arrows, he consults the teraphim, he looks at the liver" (Ezekiel 21:21, ESV).

Ironically, when Daniel interpreted the king's dream about the golden statue, he neatly exposed the failure of the university curriculum. He didn't use any fancy techniques learned at school. He didn't use omens or divination. He simply prayed to Yahweh.

Living in Babylon

The psalmist captures a poignant moment as Jewish exiles sit beside Babylonian rivers, lamenting a lost Jerusalem—alienated emotionally, physically, and spiritually from their home. Their captors command them to sing, but they cry out, "How shall we sing the LORD's song in a strange land?" (Psalm 137:1–4, KJV). This is a fundamental missiological question. How *do* we sing God's song in new and unfamiliar territories, among different cultural and religious groups, in large metropolises where we don't feel at home, where we haven't yet found our voice? How do we sing the Lord's song in modern-day Babylon?

We can count on one thing. Babylon never lasts. The ancient city of Babylon symbolizes all that opposes the city of God, Jerusalem. It's a city of sin, apostasy, and every form of degradation. In words that echo Isaiah

21:9, Revelation describes an angel delivering this message with a "mighty voice": "Fallen, fallen is Babylon the Great!" (Revelation 18:2, ESV). The warning is clear, "Come out of her, my people, lest you take part in her sins" (verse 4, ESV).

Daniel and his friends couldn't physically "come out" of Babylon. They were captives. The dilemma they faced is one that has challenged God's followers throughout history. When forced into an environment hostile to your beliefs and practices, how do you remain faithful? How can you be an effective witness? How do you conduct mission in the Babylons of this world?

The exiles had options. The first was probably the easiest. Banished as they were from their home base and its spiritual support, corporate worship with fellow Jews was only a memory. They could easily just drift into Babylonian life, its culture and its practices. Forget their Jewish heritage and Yahweh and adopt the Babylonian way of life. That way, there would be no problems with Sabbath keeping, dietary requirements, or worship.

The second option would be to remain Jewish in name but adapt to the new cultural environment. Surely God would understand that it was impossible to keep the Sabbath the same way they did at home. He would understand if occasionally they had to stay at their desks in the Babylonian administrative offices for an hour or two after sunset Friday. He would understand the impossibility of eating kosher food in a pagan city.

Clearly, many of the exiles chose one of these two options. Recent discoveries of cuneiform tablets reveal the lives of some exiles. Nearly fifty texts were written in a place between the Tigris and Euphrates Rivers called Al-Yahudu, or "Judah Town." These texts open a window into the lives of exiles only twenty-five years after Daniel and his friends were taken to Babylon—just fifteen years after the temple was destroyed. Laurie Pearce, from the University of California, Berkeley, helped translate the cuneiform into English. Commenting on one Judah Town family line that can be traced through various cuneiform sources, she writes, "This family's documentation demonstrates the rapid and comprehensive integration of Judeans into Babylonian life."[1] Unsurprisingly, when in 539 BC the Babylonians allowed the exiles to return home, a large number chose to remain in Babylon.

The *shalom* option

Besides apostasy or compromise, there was a third option. And that was God's option. Before we explore that, let's think a little more about the context. The natural tendency for any displaced ethnic group is to stick together. You can see this in any big city. In New York, for example, you'll find various ethnic areas known as Little Italy, Chinatown, Little India, Little Korea, and so on. As immigrants landed in New York, they naturally settled in these enclaves. Sociologically, it makes sense. As the old saying goes, "Birds of a feather flock together." You share history and culture. You understand the same language. You enjoy the same food. You're often connected through family. And last but not least, you understand one another's jokes.

The same for the Jewish exiles. How much easier it was to stay together. They could observe the seventh-day Sabbath, keep feast days, eat kosher food, and sing the songs of Zion. They could support one another in avoiding idolatrous Babylonian practices and comfort one another with shared memories and hopes.

But even though they might want to stick together in Little Judah, weep beside rivers, and sing nostalgic songs, God wants them to know that they won't be going home for another seventy years (Jeremiah 29:10). In a letter delivered to the exiles, God instructs them how He wants them to branch out and "sing the LORD's song" (Psalm 137:4, KJV) in their new alien urban environment. There are to be no Jewish enclaves. He tells them to settle down, build houses, plant gardens, and marry (verses 5, 6). And more than that. While they're in Babylon, God tells them to pray for and work for the city: "But seek the welfare [*shalom*] of the city where I have sent you into exile, and pray to the LORD on its behalf, for in its welfare [*shalom*] you will find your welfare [*shalom*]" (verse 7, ESV).

Shalom is one of those rich, multilayered Hebrew words that's so beautiful you almost want to hug it. It means, among other things, peace, prosperity, welfare, and wholeness. God tells the exiles to pray and work for the shalom of the city. In doing so, He says, they'll find their own shalom. This is startling counsel. They're not to set up a separate Jewish district in Babylon. Instead, they're to engage in Babylonian society to bring *shalom* to the city. And that's exactly what Daniel and his three friends do. By taking on various political and civic responsibilities in Babylon, they placed themselves in positions of influence where they could effectively work for the *shalom* of that great city (Daniel 1:18–21; 2:48, 49; 3:30; 5:29).

Far from Jerusalem, in the heart of Babylon, these young Jewish men refused to assimilate and accommodate. Instead, while following the instruction in Jeremiah's letter, they separated themselves from pagan idolatry. Many years later, Jesus would pray that His followers be in the world but not of the world. Daniel and his friends were in Babylon, but not of it. They maintained their witness to the one true God.

Blessing today's cities

In many ways, we live in a world that's quite different from ancient Babylon. But the challenge of being a witness in the great cities of the world has only become greater. According to researchers, on Wednesday, May 23, 2007, most of the world's population lived in urban areas for the first time.[2] The United Nations estimates that by 2050, 68 percent of all people will be living in cities.[3] Welcome to our new mission field.

The letter Jeremiah wrote to the exiles of Babylon contains the only specific instruction on urban ministry in the Bible. Seeking the *shalom* of our cities should be one of our highest priorities as Seventh-day

Adventists. The official mission statement of our church lists its major tasks as Christlike living, communicating, discipling, teaching, healing, and serving. Under "healing," it states, "Affirming the biblical principles of the well-being of the whole person, we make the healthful living and the healing of the sick a priority and through our ministry to the poor and oppressed, cooperate with the Creator in His compassionate work of restoration."[4]

Imagine if, today, we earnestly prayed for and worked for the *shalom* of our cities. City parks would be cleaner because Seventh-day Adventists were praying for and working for the *shalom* of the city. Streets would be safer, children better educated, and families healthier. The hope we have in Jesus would be demonstrated and not just talked about.

---

1. Laurie E. Pearce, "Cuneiform Sources for Judeans in Babylonia in the Neo-Babylonian and Achaemenid Periods: An Overview," *Religion Compass* 10, no. 9 (September 2016): 230–243.

2. North Carolina State University, "Mayday 23: World Population Becomes More Urban Than Rural," Science Daily, May 25, 2007, www.sciencedaily.com/releases/2007/05/070525000642.htm.

3. "68 Percent of the World Population Projected to Live in Urban Areas by 2050, Says UN," News, United Nations, Department of Economic and Social Affairs, May 16, 2018, https://www.un.org/development/desa/en/news/population/2018-revision-of-world-urbanization-prospects.html.

4. "Mission Statement of the Seventh-day Adventist Church," Seventh-day Adventist Church, accessed February 15, 2023, https://www.adventist.org/official-statements/mission-statement-of-the-seventh-day-adventist-church/.

12

Mission Multiplied

A world-famous classical violinist stood inside L'Enfant Plaza metro station in Washington, DC, holding his $3.5 million Stradivarius. It was a cold winter's day, and Joshua Bell began with the technically demanding "Chaconne" from J. S. Bach's Partita no. 2 in D Minor. For the next forty-three minutes, he performed six majestic classical pieces. During the entire time, a grand total of seven people stopped to listen at least for a minute—another 1,090 walked by, blissfully unaware of the musical genius among them.

Bell was busking* as part of a *Washington Post* experiment to see how people would react. Twenty-seven people gave money, for a total of $32.17. Bell later joked that $40 an hour wasn't so bad, considering. "I could make an okay living doing this," he said with a laugh, "and I wouldn't have to pay an agent." But he did admit, again with a laugh: "It was a strange feeling, that people were actually, ah . . . *ignoring* me."[1]

Being a Christian witness in non-Christian and post-Christian societies can feel like busking to deaf ears in a metro station. We understand the

---

* Busking is the act of entertaining on the street in a public place for voluntary donations.

biblical vision of being a light reaching to the ends of the earth, but sometimes we have trouble sharing the good news to the ends of our streets. We play the beautiful melody of the gospel, but few seem to listen. We try playing louder, softer, with greater virtuosity and different variations—but people still rush past, tuned to their own agendas.

Talking about the experience later, Bell said he felt a bit nervous—"there were butterflies." He's played before royalty in Europe, so why would he feel anxiety in a Washington metro station? He explained that when he plays in a concert hall, people pay for their tickets. He never feels like he must try to be accepted. But at the metro station, he was thinking, "What if they don't like me? What if they resent my presence . . . ?"[2]

Of course, the worst-case scenario for Bell was an embarrassing hour at a metro station. Likewise, when standing as a witness for God, usually, the worst-case scenario is being rejected. But in certain places and at certain times, the stakes can be much higher. The apostle Paul was beaten, thrown into prison, and eventually martyred. Queen Esther, centuries earlier, risked death by revealing her identity. In Babylon, Daniel was thrown to the lions for his faithfulness. Shadrach, Meshach, and Abednego were thrown into a fiery furnace for theirs.

The farmer went out to sow

Jesus tells a story about a farmer who went out to sow. Some seeds missed the good soil. Some landed on the path, some hit rocky places, some landed in shallow soil, and some fell into thorns.

Likewise, Joshua Bell went out to play. Even though he was playing extremely loudly in a confined space, some people didn't hear him. One man was listening to rock music through earphones. Others were busy talking loudly on their cell phones. Bell's music fell, as it were, on the path and in rocky places. Some pedestrians later remembered hearing the music, but they were so busy rushing with their own agendas that it passed through one ear and out the other.

When the farmer goes out to sow, he knows that not all the seeds will take root, grow, and flourish. But he sows anyway because he's focused on the good soil. Likewise, the job of the Christian isn't to germinate the seed—that's the role of the Holy Spirit. Our responsibility, like the farmer's, is to sow the seed (Matthew 13:3). Like Joshua Bell, we're to play the melody.

A little child shall lead them

Perhaps the most touching thing is how Joshua Bell affected children in the subway station. The children were the good soil. As he played, every child who walked past tried to stop and watch. And every single time, a parent pulled the kid away. Jesus once said that unless we become as little children, we'll never enter the kingdom of heaven. Just as those kids wanted to listen to Joshua Bell, many children at heart of all ages are just waiting to hear the old, old melody.

We play the music of the gospel in many ways. We can play through public evangelistic meetings, literature, TV programs, and the internet. But no music is more powerful than a dedicated, committed follower of Jesus who follows His method of ministry. There's no more powerful witness than a Christian who mingles with unbelievers, shows them sympathy, ministers to their needs, wins their confidence, and bids them to follow Jesus.

Interestingly, Jesus rarely did His "bidding" in what we would consider a "forward" or "clear" way. When He talked with Nicodemus, He spoke about things such as "being born again." When he spoke to the woman at the well, it was all about "the water of life." Often His words completely baffled His disciples. Why couldn't He just come straight out and say what He meant?

Magic baptism

Many years ago, when I was working at the Adventist Media Centre in

Australia, we were commissioned to make a video that would encourage teenagers to be baptized. We thought it was important to surprise the teenagers, capture their attention, and make them think. So, we followed Jesus' example of telling a parable. Our parable included a mysterious figure we called Mr. X.

Mr. X witnessed a teenage boy become a Christian and get baptized. He was intrigued when he saw the boy's life radically change. He wondered whether there might be miraculous properties in the water. So, he ordered some of his minions to gather water samples and test them in a laboratory. The idea, of course, was to show there's nothing magical or mystical about baptism—it's simply a public declaration that we have committed our lives to Jesus and want to follow Him. The details of the video are a bit hazy in my memory, but I do remember filming actors wearing scuba tanks in the baptismal font!

I pitched the script to a group of church leaders. Almost all responded enthusiastically. They believed the video would connect with teens and help them think seriously about baptism. One leader, however, wasn't impressed. "Just preach the Word," he said. "Let the Word speak." I don't disagree with what he said. We do need to preach the Word and let it speak. But the question is, How can we maximize the chance that people will listen?

The Bible, of course, speaks in many different and creative ways. You can sing your way through much of it. It's not just a collection of propositions, doctrines, and "truths." It's full of poetry, prophecy, song, story, and parable. It has rivers and trees clapping their hands (Psalm 98:8; Isaiah 55:12), mountains shouting for joy (Psalm 98:8), stars singing together (Job 38:7), tongues strutting across the earth (Psalm 73:9), wisdom calling in the street (Proverbs 1:20), water being drawn from the wells of salvation (Isaiah 12:3), and a menagerie of strange and weird beasts. It also describes Jesus the Vine (John 15:5), the Shepherd (John 10:11), the Bread of Life (John 6:35), and the Water of Life (John 4:14). And when the Bible addresses the vexed issue of theodicy, how an all-powerful and good God can allow good people to suffer, it doesn't give us a philosophical or theological treatise. It addresses the problem through Job, a book of poetry.

Truth through the back door

We do need to let the Word speak. At times Jesus spoke "straight," usually to the religious leaders. But this wasn't His regular approach. He mostly answered questions with questions, rarely with a direct answer. In fact, in the Gospels, He asks more than three hundred questions, far more than He answers. Of course, in answering questions with questions, He reflects the Jewish tradition of religious teaching through stories. "Judaism is largely based on and communicated through tales," writes Yitzhak Buxbaum. "The Torah has two parts: instruction about commandments, and stories."[3]

"[Jesus'] primary method of creating meaning was through metaphor, simile, parable and dramatic action rather than through logic and reasoning. He created meaning like a dramatist and a poet rather than like a philosopher."[4] That doesn't mean Jesus' teachings were less profound. On the contrary, it's just a Western assumption that logical reasoning and argumentation are more legitimate or effective than teaching through story. Jesus never spoke without telling a story, a parable, which sneaked truth in the back door of His listeners' minds and hearts (Mark 4:34).

Telling it slant

Christians engaged in mission to the ends of the earth quickly discover that truth must be slanted, but not compromised, to reach people in different situations. Think of the apostle Paul quoting pagan poets on Mars Hill (Acts 17:22–31). Although Paul knew how to preach straight, he also knew how to adapt his approach to his audience.

Jesus, Paul, and much of the Bible demonstrate what poet Emily Dickinson wrote:

Tell all the truth but tell it slant—
Success in Circuit lies
Too bright for our infirm Delight
The Truth's superb surprise.[5]

The Psalms tell it slant. Daniel and Revelation tell it slant. Jesus tells it slant. There are many reasons for coming at the truth from an angle. It can be more interesting and compelling. It breaks down defenses. People who would never listen to a sermon can be reached through a story. And as Dickinson concludes her poem: "The Truth must dazzle gradually / Or every man be blind."

How do we present the gospel? In abstract, clinical terms? In mere intellectual statements? In lifeless propositions? Or do we reflect our Lord, who spoke worlds into existence, turned water into wine, and never spoke without telling a parable? Throughout history, the gospel has gone "as a light to the nations" (Isaiah 51:4) because men and women have found fresh wineskins for telling the old, old story. And almost inevitably, they have faced opposition and criticism.

In 1929, H. M. S. Richards pioneered religious radio programming with the *Voice of Prophecy* broadcast. It was a radically new approach to ministry for the Seventh-day Adventist Church. Many people, including church leaders, weren't happy. Some said it was wrong because the radio advertised alcohol and cigarettes. Others conducted an imaginative exegesis on Paul's description of Satan as "prince of the power of the air" (Ephesians 2:2, KJV) and applied it to the radio. Several conferences banned *Voice of Prophecy* from their territories. Elder Richards, though, didn't think twice about using any medium to preach the gospel. "If I had a chance to preach in Rome and the Pope was in the audience, I'd jump at it," he said. "I'd love to go to the Vatican and give a series of morning devotionals."[6]

In 1950, William and Virginia Fagal launched the first Adventist television program, *Faith for Today*. Within a few months, it became the first coast-to-coast religious broadcast in North America. In some ways, it was even more daring than the launch of the *Voice of Prophecy* twenty years earlier, and it almost died an early death. The Fagals broadcast from the New York studios of WABC TV, one of America's major television networks. They started with a preaching program, but the studio directors told them, "Don't preach." Instead, they advised the use of dramatic techniques to tell true-to-life stories. Soon the Fagals were including such sketches in their programs.

For many, this was a bridge too far. Even though, along with the dramatic story there was a sermonette, "sacred" music, and advertising for Bible correspondence courses, many Adventists were outraged. At the 1952 General Conference Annual Council, speakers rose to attack the program. When it came to a vote, only 2 out of more than 150 delegates voted to keep funding it. Unusually, the chair chose not to declare the vote but continued the discussion. He then invited Elder Fagal to speak about the ministry of *Faith for Today* and the results they were seeing. Two other leaders then stood up to defend the program, and a second vote was taken. This time the vote was exactly reversed—two against and the rest in favor. The chair chose to declare the second vote![7]

Dead men do tell tales

In the 1940s, evangelist John Coltheart tried a creative new approach to public evangelism while pastoring in New Zealand. A young pastor, then in his midtwenties, Coltheart advertised the theme "Dead Men Do Tell Tales" for his opening night. The idea was to use archaeology to help prove the veracity of the Bible. "The conference president was horrified that the topic was not on heaven, or some other biblical theme, but when the hall was filled to overflowing on the first night, he withdrew his objections."[8]

In 1958 Coltheart explained to church leaders in America:

I did a little experimenting myself about thirteen years ago. I was searching around for some new approach for evangelism. Subjects such as Bible lands, archeology and the Bible, suggested a new approach. We advertised a meeting, and three conference evangelists said to me, "You won't get anybody out because Pastor So-and-So tried that approach here five years ago, and it just doesn't work." Well, I am happy to say that approach did work, and it has since been used by many of our men. I use the title "Dead Men Do Tell Tales." . . . We have gathered huge crowds with that title.[9]

A few years later, Coltheart used the method in London, England. The result was unprecedented. Phone lines rang busy for three days with people booking seats for the program, and more than eight thousand people attended on the first two days. Here's one description of the new approach: "Preceding the slide lecture proper the audiences are taken on conducted tours through many places of the Middle East and Australasia by way of scenic slides and movie films to a background of descriptive organ and piano music."[10]

I grew up in Australia attending such meetings, which we called "missions." Public evangelists would rent the town hall or some other large venue in cities across Australia and New Zealand and draw large crowds using Coltheart's approach. However, as TV was introduced in Australia, the numbers coming to these meetings declined.

A layperson with experience in TV production decided to do something about it. He personally funded seven public evangelists to travel with him to the Middle East. There, he filmed each pastor speaking in various places of interest. He then produced five different thirty-second TV ads that they could use, on rotation, before their opening night.

The first twenty seconds of the script of one of these ads went like this: "I'm [insert name] in Egypt, and this is the bearded queen, the mystery woman of ancient Egypt. Who was she? Did she really have a beard? Why did pharaoh disfigure her face, and why was her mummy the only one missing? I'll answer those questions and more at [insert name of venue] this weekend."

The on-location images were framed to include a phone number in the bottom quarter of the screen. This graphic appeared five seconds after the ad started and remained there until the end. After the on-location video, the ad cut to a graphic for the last ten seconds (with the phone number still in place). A professional voice announced the meeting's time and location details and invited people to call for free tickets.

"We had 12,500 attend in Melbourne, and 17,000 in the Sydney Opera House," the layperson who funded and produced the ads said. "We got so many baptisms that the increase in tithe paid for the entire evangelistic campaign in two years." The simple innovation of filming the evangelists on-site in biblical lands gave them a huge boost in public credibility.

Since Coltheart trialed the archaeological approach, it has led tens of thousands of people around the world to baptisms. His method is still used, although in some places it now struggles to get a crowd. But it's easy to overlook how innovative and groundbreaking this approach was.

Untried methods

Sadly, we often see a lack of creativity and innovation in mission. Many Christian bookshops in America symbolize the problem. Most books they carry are aimed at Christians—saints talking to saints. And if you're looking for something that seriously engages mission, you'll have trouble. First, you have to navigate your way past Christian T-shirts, jewelry, Testamints, Christian weight-loss books, celebrity biographies, and a veritable claustrophobe of self-help books. And make sure you don't trip over the health-and-wealth tomes on your way out.

Of course, it's natural that Christian bookstores will sell products aimed at Christians. But shouldn't they also help equip Christians to engage with unbelievers and their communities more effectively? It's almost as if we've given up on impacting our wider culture. Instead, we live and move and have our being entirely within the Christian subculture. And when someone bravely moves out to try new and creative ways to engage nonbelievers, they're often shot down in pious flames of criticism. "We've never done it that way before." "You're watering down the truth." "Just preach the Word!"

Light to the nations

In July 1849, a young James White produced the first issue of an eight-page paper called *Present Truth*—the result of hard labor, experimentation, and sacrifice. He printed just a thousand copies. But they were part of a large, bold vision. The year before, his wife, Ellen, dreamed of a small paper that would grow into "streams of light that went clear round the world."[11] Light to the nations, indeed.

But by December, White stopped printing. Funds were running low; he was discouraged. Making matters worse, Joseph Bates gave him no support. Fellow cofounder of the Adventist Church and the most senior Adventist preacher alive, Bates even refused to write for the publication. He felt White shouldn't be messing around wasting time on newfangled methods of witness when the funding should go to direct evangelism.

Many external factors can block Isaiah's vision of light going to the nations. But too often, the blockages come from within—focusing on maintenance rather than mission, protecting the "way we've always done it," clinging to what's most comfortable. Fortunately, come spring, White found the courage and means to continue, and Adventist publishing was born.[12]

Many years later, Ellen White wrote: "Whatever may have been your former practice, it is not necessary to repeat it again and again in the same way. God would have new and untried methods followed. Break in upon the people—surprise them."[13] And you can almost hear the frustration in her voice when she said, "But somebody must venture; someone must run risks in this cause."[14]

Like Joshua Bell at the metro station, there's no guarantee that everybody will stop to listen to the old, old melody. But we're called to keep playing anyway.

---

1. Gene Weingarten, "Pearls Before Breakfast," *Washington Post*, April 8, 2007; italics in original.

2. Weingarten.

3. Yitzhak Buxbaum, *Storytelling and Spirituality in Judaism* (Lanham, MD: Rowman and Littlefield, 1994), xv.

4. Kenneth E. Bailey, *Jesus Through Middle Eastern Eyes* (Downers Grove, IL: InterVarsity Press, 2008), 279.

5. Emily Dickinson, "Tell All the Truth but Tell It Slant," Poetry Foundation, accessed February 20, 2023, https://www.poetryfoundation.org/poems/56824/tell-all-the-truth-but-tell-it-slant-1263.

6. John Robertson, "The Voice of H.M.S. Richards," *Spectrum* 13, no. 1 (September 1982): 41.

7. Dan Shultz, "Faith for Today," *Encyclopedia of Seventh-day Adventists*, November 28, 2021, https://encyclopedia.adventist.org/article?id=8JHM&highlight=y.

8. Michelle Down, "Coltheart, John Frederick (1924–1974)," *Encyclopedia of Seventh-day Adventists*, January 29, 2020, https://encyclopedia.adventist.org/article?id=G7UU&highlight=coltheart.

9. R. A. Anderson et al., "Overseas Evangelism Rally," *Ministry*, November 1958, https://www.ministrymagazine.org/archive/1958/11/overseas-evangelism-rally.

10. Malcolm Taylor, "The Greater London Evangelistic Campaign," *The British Advent Messenger* 70, no. 22 (October 22, 1965): 2.

11. Ellen G. White, *The Publishing Ministry* (Hagerstown, MD: Review and Herald®, 1983), 16.

12. George Knight, *Joseph Bates: The Real Founder of Adventism* (Hagerstown, MD: Review and Herald®, 2004), 162–164.

13. Ellen G. White, *Evangelism* (Washington, DC: Review and Herald®, 1946), 125.

14. White, 688.

13

The End of God's Mission

Michael Stifel, a Protestant reformer and friend of Martin Luther, was a remarkable and innovative mathematician. In 1532 he applied his skills to the book of Revelation. In a pamphlet titled *An Arithmetic Book of the Antichrist: Revelation of the Apocalypse*, Stifel declared that the end of the world was near. Soon after it was published, he fine-tuned his calculations and pinpointed the exact time—8:00 AM on Wednesday, October 19, 1533.

Setting dates for the Second Coming is never a great idea. Luther tried to talk him out of it, but Stifel went ahead and publicly announced his findings. Trusting their pastor, many of Stifel's faithful church members sold everything and resigned from their jobs. When October 19 passed as just another normal day, the failed forecaster was fired and jailed. A harsh punishment for a little mathematical tinkering with prophecy.

This wasn't Stifel's first venture into creative biblical interpretation. Some years earlier, he made another startling claim—he identified Martin Luther as the angel of Revelation 14:6, 7. The idea must have caught on because, nearly a quarter of a century later, it was mentioned at Luther's funeral. Johann Bugenhagen, the Wittenberg pastor, said:

He was without doubt the angel concerning whom it is written in Revelation 14, who flew through the midst of heaven and had an eternal Gospel. . . .

This angel who says, "Fear God and give him the honor," was Dr. Martin Luther. And what is written here, "Fear God and give him the honor," are the two parts of Dr. Martin Luther's doctrine, the Law and the Gospel, through which all Scripture is unlocked and Christ, our righteousness and eternal life, is recognized.[1]

Luther's friends were well-intentioned but wrong. He didn't qualify as the angel of Revelation 14:6. The three flying angels in this chapter are missionaries from heaven. They symbolize spreading the truth about God's character and the good news of salvation throughout the world. Luther was certainly a vital part of promoting that message, but he wasn't an angel.

Angels of salvation

Throughout Revelation, angels work nonstop as God's agents for salvation. They're everywhere, flying in and out of the entire book. They descend from heaven, fly in midair, encircle the throne of God, hold back the winds of strife, cry in loud voices, seize dragons, measure cities, deliver messages, offer incense, blow trumpets, and pour out bowls. One angel even acts as a tour guide to the New Jerusalem (Revelation 21:10).

The first of the three missionary angels of Revelation 14 proclaims the good news of "the eternal gospel" (verse 6). The Greek verb used for that proclamation, *euangelizō*, means "to announce," "to preach," or "to bring good news." It means much more than our modern picture of someone standing up and preaching. It's used when the angels at Jesus' birth "bring . . . good news" to Zechariah (Luke 1:19, NLT) and "bring . . . good news" of great joy to the shepherds (Luke 2:10). These angels at Jesus' birth do the same thing as the angel in Revelation 14. They serve as couriers of God's good news.

The good news of Revelation 14 isn't for a select group of people—it's for every "nation, tribe, language and people" (verse 6). That effectively covers the eight billion people living on the earth. The message also isn't for a specific time—it's an "eternal gospel" (verse 6). However, it does grow more urgent and compelling in the last days of the earth's history.

It's particularly relevant in a world where God's character is increasingly slandered, even, at times, by His followers. For example, award-winning author Frank McCourt describes what it was like to grow up in Ireland: "We didn't hear much about a loving God. We were told God is good and that was supposed to be enough. . . . Our God had a stern face. When He wasn't writhing up there on the cross in the shape of His Son, He had His priests preaching hellfire and damnation from the pulpit and scaring us to death. . . . We were told shut up, drink your tea, stop asking questions."[2]

This impression of God gives a bad name to the One that "loves us and has freed us from our sins by his blood" (Revelation 1:5), the One who is worthy of praise and worship because "salvation and glory and power" belong to Him, and "true and just are his judgments" (Revelation 19:1, 2). In a beautiful image, John describes the missionary Jesus knocking on the door of our lives. If we listen and open the door, He will join us and fellowship with us. He seeks, loves, and saves the lost (Revelation 3:20).

The great controversy

Revelation sings with symbols, metaphors, and poetry. It's a colorful book full of choirs, elders falling on their faces to worship, trumpets sounding. It pulls back the curtain and gives us glimpses of a universe we know little about. Amid rising smoke and incense, dragons being hurled to the earth, and beasts coming out of the sea emerges a beautiful truth: a loving God, in and above all, is working nonstop for the salvation of His creation.

This simple truth often gets lost and forgotten in various interpretations and speculations about Revelation: it's primarily a book about mission. It's about God triumphing in a universal spiritual war between the forces of evil and the forces of righteousness. And it's about how God, in the process, seeks to save as many people as possible.

The cosmic war isn't just some theoretical concept. It cuts deeply into the battleground of every human heart. Any effective witness today must engage and speak to this tension. The apostle John tells us that God lights everyone who comes into the world (John 1:9). Every choice we make from birth to death either brightens that light or dims it. God created us in His image, but our choices either sharpen or blur that image. We may not even realize it, but we all end up worshiping somebody or something. Our mission, as Jesus' followers, is to help strengthen the light in every life. To help direct people from false worship to true worship (Revelation 14:9–12).

Facing both ways

Some people try to have a foot on each side of the cosmic conflict, like a character in *The Pilgrim's Progress* who is called Mr. Facing-both-ways. It's a great name but a most uncomfortable position to be in. He personifies what Jesus once said: "No one can serve two masters" (Matthew 6:24).

We see this with Demas, a Greek convert to Christianity, who was a great friend of the apostle Paul. Demas traveled with Paul, stayed close to him during his first imprisonment, and was one of Paul's "fellow workers" (Philemon 24). But sadly, Demas proved to be a Mr. Facing-both-ways.

While in prison and awaiting death, Paul wrote to Timothy and mentioned Demas. It's one of the most chilling and one of the saddest verses in all of Scripture. "For Demas," Paul writes, "in love with this present world, has deserted me" (2 Timothy 4:10, ESV). I imagine

Paul dictating those words through tears of pain. His faithful friend, fellow church planter, and brother in mission deserted him because of his love of the world. He was another casualty in the great controversy between good and evil.

Revelation assures us that, in the great cosmic conflict, Babylon will ultimately fall along with all its pride, cruelty, and false forms of worship. God will triumph. In the meantime, we're called to *euangelizō* the truth about God and His unfailing love for His creation. But even more important, we're called to *demonstrate* that truth.

As we draw closer to the end of time, the key themes of the great controversy will be painted in even more vivid colors. The contrast between God's kingdom and Satan's kingdom will become more clearly delineated. Those opposing God will become bolder, their rhetoric more inflamed. Those on God's side will become more committed, aligning themselves more closely to His will.

But in some ways, the lines will blur. Many who claim the name of Jesus will oppose freedom, a key value of God's kingdom, and try to force their views on others. They'll obscure rather than demonstrate the loving and compassionate character of God. And many who've never set foot in a church will more closely reveal the fundamental principles of God's kingdom.

In the end labels won't count. Membership on a church roll will mean virtually nothing. God will raise His end-time movement among all those who have responded to His call. A call that has echoed in highways and byways. A call that has gone to Jerusalem, Samaria, and to the uttermost ends of the earth. From the east to the west, north to the south. Among the rich and poor, the young and old, among men and women. His true remnant will emerge from prisons and palaces, churches and mosques, factories and offices, shacks, and mansions. They'll be speaking different languages, and they'll have different skin colors. But they'll be keeping the commandments of God and clinging to the faith of Jesus (Revelation 14:12). Some in that group will have never heard the name of Jesus. But they'll be ready to give glory to Him. They'll hear the mission call to leave Babylon with all its misunderstanding and confusion, its blasphemy and sin. They'll say yes to the call to worship Him who made heaven and earth and the sea and springs of water.

Faithfulness and discipleship

This book began with the story of a mother desperately searching for her lost son. That story ended happily when they were reunited after more than three decades. But for many parents, this hasn't been their experience—likewise with God. The cosmic war rages today because God has given every human being the power of free choice. Sadly, some will exercise their free choice and stay with Babylon.

Even God can't make salvation a 100 percent success story. "The prosperity gospel is a wildly popular Christian message of spiritual, physical, and financial mastery that dominates not only much of the American religious scene but some of the largest churches around the globe." This message guarantees "a special form of Christian power to reach into God's treasure trove and pull out a miracle."[3] Basically, this gospel teaches that if you have enough faith, God will always bless you with good things, such as health and wealth.

As Seventh-day Adventists, we've done a pretty good job of avoiding the bad theology of the prosperity gospel. But we need to be cautious. We love wonderful Bible stories of God's presence, His immediacy, and His marvelous interventions. We love to hear miracles stories and mission stories with happy endings and many baptisms. And so we should. Heaven does too (Luke 15:7). But these stories aren't the full story. If we're not careful, a type of mission prosperity gospel can creep into our mission and lead us to focus on "success" rather than on faithfulness, commitment, and discipleship. It's tempting to focus on the big baptisms and marvelously successful evangelistic meetings while missing the larger story of mission.[4]

That larger story involves sacrifice, tears, disappointments, mind-numbing challenges, and a world where most people still don't know Jesus.

Too often, the way we speak belittles pastors and church members in challenging mission fields such as Australia, the Middle East, or Europe. Sometimes we imply that they would have more baptisms if they had more faith, used better methods, or prayed harder.

Preaching to the angels

Some years ago, during his retirement, my father pastored a country church in Australia. I visited once when he was starting a series of public evangelistic meetings. The church had placed advertisements in local newspapers. Every house in the town had received a handbill. And it was opening night.

Dad and I arrived early at the church to prepare. But as the starting time drew closer, nobody had come. Fifteen minutes to go, and still nobody. Ten minutes, nobody. Five minutes, nobody. At starting time, Dad asked me to see if someone was waiting at a different door. Sure enough, there was nobody. That story didn't make the cover of the *Adventist Review*.

Some years later, I later heard about a Global Mission pioneer in Russia by the name of Vadim Kibe. This young man was trying to plant a new church in Kostroma, a historic city on the Volga River. He carefully planned a series of public outreach meetings. On the first night, seven people attended. On the second night, only four. On the third night, nobody came. The hall was empty except for Vadim. Undeterred, on that unforgettable night, Vadim stood up and preached to 160 empty chairs. "I imagined that in every chair there was an angel," he said, "and that 160 angels were looking at me and crying with me."[5]

What a wonderful thing if the whole town had turned up to my father's meetings. What a blessing if there had been standing room only during Vadim's meetings. But it wasn't to be. And please don't try to tell me that if Vadim and my father had more faith, they would have seen baptisms. Their experience may have been discouraging, but in the eyes of God, their commitment was no less than those of a famous evangelist preaching to a stadium of ten thousand people.

There were times in the Bible when mighty people of faith felt discouraged. Habakkuk asked God why He didn't listen (Habakkuk 1:1, 2), Jeremiah asked Him why He was "like a mighty man who cannot save" (Jeremiah 14:9, RSV), and even Jesus cried out: "My God, my God, why have you forsaken me?" (Matthew 27:46).

I often think of my father waiting hopefully for my report from the church door. I think of that humble pioneer, standing in an empty hall and preaching his heart out to the angels, tears streaming down his face. Their faithfulness impresses me as much as inspiring baptismal reports from the Philippines or Papua New Guinea or the southern half of the continent of Africa. We rejoice to see God's kingdom growing quickly in certain parts of the world. But that should never diminish or outshine what faithful people are doing in other areas.

Prosperity gospel theology doesn't mix well with mission. We're called to be His witnesses. We're called to go into all the world and make disciples. We're called to be faithful. But numbers? They belong entirely to God. And, I guess, to the General Conference Office of Archives, Statistics, and Research.

Postlude

When I was growing up in Australia and New Zealand, Marmite was always an essential part of our family's diet. Some unfortunate readers may have never had the privilege of eating a slice of hot toast with this delicious black, salty yeast spread. But don't worry. I'm sure you'll get a chance when you get to heaven.

Sadly, some American friends try it, wrinkle their noses, and act as if they're in pain. They ask me how I can eat the stuff. I can only hope that one day their palates will be converted, and they'll come to appreciate its appeal.

Marmite's main competitor is Vegemite. Vegemite was never found on our dining table. Why? Because Marmite is made by Sanitarium Health and Wellness Company, and Sanitarium is owned by the Seventh-day Adventist Church. We knew that every dollar spent on a jar of Marmite or Weet-Bix or any other Sanitarium product helped their profits. And Sanitarium profits significantly contributed to the mission program of the church in the South Pacific.

For us, a dollar spent on Vegemite or any other competitor's product was almost like pulling missionaries out of the mission field and sending them home. It would be the first step in certain apostasy. I won't say that spending money on competitors was giving money to the devil, but it seemed like it would be close.

Our unfailing support of Sanitarium may seem trivial. But it was important to me because it reflected something significant—a mission orientation in our home. This orientation also meant we prayed in family worship each day for "the missionaries in the islands." It taught my brother and me that mission should not be some sort of optional extra but be a way of life.

In this book, I've highlighted a few heroes of mine who've dedicated their lives to share the love of Jesus and to care for the poor and marginalized. But I want to also pay tribute to the tens of thousands of unnamed Adventists who, in less dramatic ways, keep the church's mission alive.

You quietly practice Christ's method of ministry in your community. You faithfully give your mission offerings every week. You pray each day for missionaries, Global Mission pioneers, tentmakers, literature evangelists, and others on the front lines of mission. You teach your children and grandchildren that service to others should be our highest priority.

Thank you for making God's mission your mission! "And let us not grow weary while doing good, for in due season we shall reap if we do not lose heart" (Galatians 6:9, NKJV). "Always give yourselves fully to the work of the Lord, because you know that your labor in the Lord is not in vain" (1 Corinthians 15:58).

---

1. Kurt K. Hendel, ed., *A Christian Sermon: Over the Body and at the Funeral of the Venerable Dr. Martin Luther, Preached by Mr. Johann Bugenhagen Pomeranus, Doctor and Pastor of the Churches in Wittenberg* (Atlanta: Pitts Theology Library, 1996), 17, 19, https://s3-us-west-2.amazonaws.com/pittspublic/publications/Hendel_Bugenhagen ChristianSermon.pdf.

2. Frank McCourt, "When You Think of God What Do You See?" *Life*, December 1998, 63.

3. Kate Bowler, *Blessed: A History of the American Prosperity Gospel* (New York: Oxford University Press, 2013), 3, 7.

4. Sometimes we measure the success of evangelistic meetings only in terms of baptisms. However, the high apostasy rate in the Adventist Church should motivate us to measure the effectiveness of these meetings also in terms of long-term discipleship.

5. Vadim later held more meetings and established an Adventist congregation in Kostroma.